Directions for Disciples

Studies in the Gospel of Luke

"A disciple is not above the teacher, but everyone
who is fully qualified will be like the teacher."

– Luke 6:40

Tony Ash

DIRECTIONS FOR DISCIPLES: STUDIES IN THE GOSPEL OF LUKE

HillCrest
PUBLISHING

1648 Campus Court
Abilene, TX 79601

Cover design by Fritz Miller. Typesetting by Mark Houston.
© 2002 Tony Ash

Printed in the United States of America

ISBN 0-89112-486-1

Library of Congress Card Number 2002100818

1,2,3,4,5

TABLE OF
■ Contents

CHAPTER 1
■ Introduction

I did not grow up going to church, so when I became a Christian I found myself in a new world. I knew I wanted to follow Jesus, but wasn't sure what kind of behavior that would require. I knew the general teachings most folks are aware of (be honest, stay sober, keep your speech clean, go to church, etc.), but I wondered if there were other things to know and practice. I even thought the Christians might have had some secret rules they trotted out once you were "in."

Granted, I was pretty ignorant of Christian basics but, because of my ignorance, one of the things I most wanted to know was exactly what form my journey with Jesus should take. I wanted concrete information. Just exactly what does a disciple of Jesus do? How is the Christian life to be lived? What are the dos and don'ts? What attitudes are important to have and to avoid?

I suppose that Christians in the early days of the faith had similar questions, and even those who didn't needed to have reminders and encouragements as their faith faced problems and opposition.

This book is about being a disciple of Jesus. This was an urgent concern for me in those early days of my pilgrimage and it is still urgent today, though I trust I know a bit more now than I did then. I don't need to justify talking about discipleship; those who are serious about Jesus' "follow me" will always want all the information they can get. They will also need and want help in being what they are called to be.

Because of this concern, there will always be an interest in the topic of discipleship. In fact, it has been the topic of a number of books in recent years. There has also been a great stress in many quarters on the process of "discipling";

techniques for it have been advocated and employed. They have achieved some success and sometimes generated some controversy. In fact, in some cases, it has seemed as if "discipling" has taken on a life of its own, even at the expense of losing a vital connection with Jesus.

It is clear, however, that this concern for producing dedicated disciples was uppermost in the minds of many, if not all, of the New Testament writers. That certainly was the case with Luke. The directions for disciples discussed here are Jesus' directions mediated to us through Luke. I invite you to prepare for a journey through this most beautiful of the gospels. Come with an inquiring mind—ready to learn—and an inquiring life—ready to practice.

Often when we read or study our Bibles we look at a given passage in detail and ponder its meaning. This is important. But also important is another view that is frequently overlooked. What is the big picture? Why did this author write at all? Why did Luke write his gospel? Since he tells us up front that others had written before him (1:1-4), why did he add to the list? What did he mean when he said he was writing "the truth" to Theophilus (1:4)?

To get this big picture, we must keep in mind that a gospel writer like Luke was doing two things. First, he was telling the story of Jesus; that's the main thing we look for as we read. But second, he was telling that story to a particular set of readers who lived in a specific place, at a specific time, and with specific needs. Thus, as he was guided by God, he told the story of Jesus in such a way that it would have particular application to those readers. A parallel might be a preacher who re-preaches, in a new location, a sermon he had previously preached. He realizes that a new audience has a different social setting, different problems, and different needs. So the "old" sermon, which may be well worth repeating, needs some readjustment to the new situation. Luke knew who would read what he wrote. He knew what materials to select from the many teachings and details of the Lord's life, material that could speak effectively to his audience.

2

So, we have a big picture with two elements: one is the story of Jesus, and the second is the way it was told to fit a certain context. Now for some detective work: how do we figure out just what special emphases a gospel writer wished to convey to his readers? Most students who have been through a basic introduction to the gospels know, for example, that Matthew includes numerous touches that appealed to the Jewish mentality. Mark apparently wrote for the Romans, and thus emphasized the power and the deeds (rather than the words) of Jesus. Luke, our gospel, stresses such things as prayer, the Holy Spirit, God's love for all humanity, and joy.

But how do we discover such special touches in each gospel? One method is to read through a gospel several times so that its major ideas become obvious. For example, it is not possible to read Luke without noting how often he speaks of wealth and poverty, or to notice how often God's love for the lost comes to center stage.

But beyond these more obvious things, a great deal can be learned by comparing Luke with Matthew and Mark—especially with Mark. A good gospel parallel is very helpful in this comparison (cf. *Gospel Parallels* edited by H. Burton Throckmorton). Many scholars assume that the first of our gospels was written by Mark, and that both Luke and Matthew knew Mark and used his basic outline as they wrote. On this comparative basis, then, we can look at all the material found only in Luke. There is a lot of it, including many of the best-loved gospel stories. If we look at this material, as well as at Luke's characteristic vocabulary, we can get an excellent sense of the special focus of this gospel.

There are other ways comparisons with Matthew and Mark help us. Sometimes there is an instructive difference in detail in a story shared with one or both of the other gospels. Sometimes a changed order of events gives insight, especially when we remember that the first and last events in a series are usually the most important. The same story may be found in different places in the progress of the

3

different gospels. For example, the story of Jesus being rejected at Nazareth is told far earlier in Luke than in Matthew and Mark, and thus plays a much more important role in the way Luke shows us Jesus (compare Luke 4:16-30 with Mark 6:1-6 and Matt. 13:53-58).

Then too, there may be passages in Mark that Luke omits. If he knew Mark's material, why did he leave some of it out? Probably because it did not fit his purpose. So, in all of this investigating, our detective work will help us see what Luke especially wants his readers to see—and much of what we see will instruct us regarding discipleship. We should remember, also, that Luke, in painting his picture, does so under God's guidance.

This kind of detective work, which I've been privileged to conduct over many years, has led to the present volume. The mystery I wanted to solve presented itself as I thought about Luke's central section, describing Jesus' journey to Jerusalem. In 9:51 we are told Jesus set his face to go to Jerusalem, and in 19:27 he came to the end of the journey. This section is unusual for several reasons. First, Luke has so much more of his text covering this travel period than does any other gospel. If you combine all the material dealing with this trip from Matthew (19:1-20:34), Mark (10:1-52) and John (12:1-19) the total is less than one third as long as the texts in Luke. Secondly, Luke's story does not seem to be interested in how far Jesus traveled each day. Travel notes are scattered, and do not always indicate direct progress toward Jerusalem. What Luke does want us to remember is that all these things were happening around a man who was on his way to die, who knew his fate, and yet went steadfastly toward it. Jesus first spoke of his death in 9:22. Then we learn from 9:31 that it was to happen ("his departure"—NIV) in Jerusalem. He spoke of it again in 9:44. So when he set out for Jerusalem (9:51) we know he went willingly to that terrible destiny. Besides other reminders, he gave a more detailed prediction of his suffering in 18:31f.

Third, most of the stories and episodes in these chapters (especially through 18:14) are found only in Luke. Here, for example, are the stories of the good Samaritan, the friend at midnight, the rich fool, the prodigal son, the unjust steward, the rich man and Lazarus, and Zacchaeus.

Because of its length and contents, and because it is clearly such an important section of the gospel, these chapters have attracted a great deal of attention among Bible students. Much has been written in an attempt to find some kind of unifying theme connecting all these materials. I do not claim to have found an answer that will satisfy all the scholars, but I hope the answer I am suggesting will inform and enrich the faith of those of you who read these words.

I have wondered if the material in these chapters might not all center on the idea of what it means to be a disciple of Jesus. Working with this hypothesis I made an analysis of all these passages to see if and how they might support such a theme. When I had finished, I concluded that all of Luke's central section *could* fit into various categories supporting the basic theme of discipleship.

It makes sense to assume that what Luke says in his central section would be of a piece with the entire gospel. For that reason, I will not limit the discussion to chapters 9:51 through 19:27. Instead, I'll take a running start from the beginning of the gospel to see how previous texts prepare readers for the central section. Then I will examine the consequences of Jesus' teaching by noting what Luke says after 19:27. It may seem at times as if a number of themes are thrown together in a helter-skelter arrangement. However, I have endeavored to select materials from whatever chapters are considered that bear on the issue of discipleship. In due time, all the strands will come together, and along the way, I'll attempt to make the connections clear.

Chapters 1 through 9:50 prepare us in many ways for the central section, as we shall see. But the central section itself is, in a way, only prologue. What would Jesus' followers do once they reached Jerusalem and experienced the dramatic events there? Would they heed his instructions? Would the call to discipleship "take?" These questions are answered in the rest of the gospel (19:28-24:53) and especially in the book of Acts (indeed, Acts is probably best understood as "Luke, Part 2"). In noticing those answers, we should learn some valuable lessons about our own faith.

Along our journey, we will be led to ask such questions as "Is Jesus one whom we should want to follow?" "What is the relation of discipleship to 'total commitment'?" "How can we deal with our failures as disciples?" "How should we relate to others whose discipleship is inadequate?" "Where do we get the power to be the disciples God has called us to be?"

The basic meaning of the word "disciple" is "a learner or pupil." It is generally agreed that the term is virtually equivalent to "Christian." One who learns from Jesus makes a commitment to be like him and is thus a disciple. Therefore, a central text in this study is Luke 6:40. As we proceed through this study, we should constantly keep before us these words of Jesus:

"A disciple is not above his teacher, but every one when he is fully taught will be like his teacher."

Since Jesus is our teacher, this verse, in a nutshell, gives the very essence of our quest. We want to be like Jesus. Just what does that involve?

DISCUSSION QUESTIONS

1. Were there any surprises about the behavior expected of you when you became a Christian?

2. What are some contemporary views of what Christian discipleship ought to be?

3. Does the idea that the contents of Luke reflected the needs of his readers open any doors for you in understanding the gospel?

4. Based on Luke 1:1-4 and your own reflection, what do you think was the situation with Luke's readers?

5. What passages in Luke 9:51 through 19:27 give geographical travel notes? Are they geographically consistent? What can we learn from this?

6. Before going further in this study, indicate what you think the central concerns and requirements of Christian discipleship should be.

CHAPTER 2
■ Luke 1:1-2:52

It will be extremely helpful to have the biblical material well in mind as our discussion unfolds. I hope you'll have an open Bible at hand as we proceed, and will refer to it often. The little extra effort can advance some insights that might otherwise be missed.

Why not stop reading this book now and spend a few minutes in a careful reading of Luke 1 and 2? Then, as we proceed into subsequent parts of the gospel we can also pause for advance readings of the passages to be discussed.

Luke 1:1-2:52

First, let's review the material in these chapters and point out some important characteristics of it. Then we'll look at some emphases that relate to the discipleship theme and show how they fit the larger picture.

Matthew and Luke both record the birth of Jesus, but the stories they tell are different. So, what Luke says in these two chapters is not found in any other source. Consequently, this unique material can lead us into some of the concepts that distinguish this gospel.

After his prologue (1:1-4), unique in the gospels, we read the story of the angel's announcement to Zechariah about the birth of John to Elizabeth (1:5-25). The same messenger later tells Mary she, though a virgin, will bear a son as well (1:26-38). Mary goes to visit the now-pregnant Elizabeth. Filled with the Spirit, Elizabeth rejoices at Mary's role in God's plan (1:39-45). Mary in turn "sings a song," known as the *Magnificat*, which celebrates these events (1:46-56). Then John is born, as promised, circumcised, and named (1:57-66). Zechariah, freed from the speechlessness earlier imposed on him for his lack of faith, also sings a song (the *Benedictus*, 1:67-79). There is a brief statement about John's growth in 1:80. Then we read the familiar story of Jesus' birth, the announcement to the shepherds, the song of the heavenly host, and the shepherds' visit to the infant in the manger (2:1-20). Jesus is circumcised (2:21), then taken to the temple where both Simon, in the *Nunc Dimittis* (2:29-35), and Anna, celebrate Jesus' coming role as Messiah (2:22-39). Two summaries about the growth of Jesus, in 2:40 and 52, bracket the story of Jesus being lost in the temple at the age of twelve (2:41-51).

Notice how these chapters show parallels between John and Jesus (births announced, births, circumcisions, the respective roles of the two, and summaries). But this is done in such a way that the superiority of Jesus is clearly shown. The story about John ends (until chapter 3) with the words of Zechariah in 1:68-79 and the following summary statement in 1:80. However, the story of Jesus continues. As was the case with John, the last statement about Jesus in these chapters is also a summary (2:52).

Luke has been called a painter with words, and his gospel has been considered the most beautiful of the four. He certainly was a master stylist, evidenced in these chapters. Since he is describing the Jewish background from which Jesus came, he writes in a manner that is reminiscent of the Septuagint. Nowhere else in his writing does Luke's material read quite the way it does here. Even in the English Bible, the change in the text is obvious as one moves into chapter 3. This evidence of Luke's skillfulness bolsters his claim that he was writing an "orderly account" (1:3) and alerts us to look carefully at the way his gospel is knit together to support his directions for disciples.

It is also important to notice how Luke depicts the centrality of God in the first two chapters. Though we meet various human characters, every episode is one in which God is the main actor. He sends an angel three times (1:11, 26f.; 2:9). He inspires speech four times (1:41f., 67; 2:27f.,

36-38) and might be presumed to inspire Mary's speech in 1:46ff. as well, since the Holy Spirit had come upon her (1:32). He makes promises (1:14-17, 20, 31-36; 2:29-35) and fulfills them (1:45, 54f., 57, 68ff.; 2:7, 26). He makes possible supernatural births (both Elizabeth's and Mary's). He brings a Messiah who will save the people (1:54ff., 68ff.; 2:11). He is obeyed and praised. He is central in the careers of John (1:66) and Jesus (2:40). A key statement is 1:37: "For with God nothing will be impossible." Such a statement will be verified throughout the gospel, as well as hold incredible promise for those who, through Jesus, would follow such a God.

It is also instructive to pay special attention to the poetic sections of these chapters (1:14-17, 32-35, 46-55, 68-79; 2:10-12, 14, and 29-35) because they carry so much of the meaning of the events that were promised and transpired. Here we find how the plans God purposed of old were being fulfilled. Here, in fact, the words are those of God himself (or of his Spirit), giving the interpretations of what was happening in these episodes. It is probably correct to see in these poetic sections the theological heart of these chapters, as well as to see themes that will color the entire gospel. Try reading just the poetic sections. Note how rich the conceptions are and how they flow together, at times almost like a single poem. Then read just the prose sections and see how much is missing and unexplained when the poetry is omitted.

The Discipleship Theme

Notice how the six main characters are described. Zechariah and Elizabeth are "both righteous before God, walking in all the commandments and ordinances of the Lord blameless" (1:6). Mary, when charged with her staggering and threatening responsibility, replied, "Behold, I am the handmaid of the Lord" (1:38). In so doing, she risked scandal, loss of Joseph, and perhaps even the penalty of the law for (supposed) adultery. Later, her faith is

11

complimented in Elizabeth's inspired speech (1:45). Joseph is described, along with Mary, as conscientious in keeping the requirements of the law (2:22-24). Simeon was "righteous and devout, looking for the consolation of Israel" (2:25). Finally, pious Anna "did not depart from the temple, worshiping with fasting and prayer night and day" (2:37).

The reason God chose such people through whom to work, and the reason Luke records it, is probably to show that the beginnings of Christianity came out of the best of the Jewish background. Though these people were not leaders of the Jews in terms of power and prestige, they did represent the best of what an Israelite ought to be; these were the kind of people God desired and used. Thus a goal is set before the reader. Later, the church would be able to point to such antecedents to bolster its claim of continuity with Israel's history, as well as to model the life of commitment to God.

However, we do notice Zechariah's lapse of faith (1:18-20, 62-64). This may be a hint of the later unbelief and immaturity of Jesus' followers (9:28-56). Perhaps Luke is showing us the ideal, but is also saying that God and Jesus chose people short of the ideal, with the intention of bringing them to the kind of maturity seen in the individuals in chapters 1 and 2. Certainly Luke will introduce us to many sinners in his gospel. He will show us how much God cares for them and how many such lives were transformed. Zechariah, though flawed, can still be God's instrument. This shows God's goal for our lives, as well as the understanding that God is loving and patient when we fall short in moving toward that goal, a great comfort.

As we might expect, we also learn something about discipleship from observing Jesus. Remember that a central verse in Luke which bears on our study is 6:40: "A disciple is not above his teacher, but every one when he is fully taught will be like his teacher." In Jesus, Luke shows us the perfect example of humanity. He is the ideal of all Christian striving. The concept is found throughout the gospel but, in the present section, is discovered in 2:41-52. First, even at the age of twelve, Jesus recognized the priority of God in his life. "Did you not know that I must be in my Father's house?" (2:49) was not only his first "adult" statement, but it also showed his special understanding of God, indicated by the term "Father." The very context of discussion with the teachers (2:46f.) and the amazement it caused indicated how much Jesus had applied himself to religious issues and how deeply he had thought about them, even in tender years. Isn't it amazing to see a twelve-year-old so concerned with such issues, and so thoughtful in considering them that his understanding and answers amazed all who heard him? Do we encourage our children to such devotion when they are very young? Do their interests reflect the same concerns Jesus had?

Further, Jesus was submissive to his parents, a point specifically indicated in verse 51. Anyone who may have thought that Jesus' previous remarks in verse 49 were impertinent is wrong. When he said, "Did you not know that I must be in my Father's house," he probably meant "knowing me and my interests, you might have known to look in the temple." Notice too that he calls God "Father." Though not unknown in the Old Testament, such a way of describing God is unusual, and probably speaks of Jesus' sense of intimate relation to God. Of course, Jesus was God. But Luke's purpose here is to see his human God-centeredness.

Finally in this text, verse 52 indicates the growth of Jesus "in wisdom and stature, and in favor with God and man." What better statement could be made of the ideal for the progress and growth of any person?

Notice that the life of Jesus can be bracketed by two statements which certainly are the measure of the man. His first recorded words are the statement about his Father's house (2:49), cited above. His last are in Luke 23:46: "Father, into thy hands I commit my spirit!" It is as if Luke tells us that all of Jesus' life between these words was a demonstration of what they expressed. If our lives were to be summed up in our first and last words, what would those words indicate about the way we had lived?

As we move through Luke, we will often encounter references to the blessings to be found in discipleship. Certainly this gospel gives us some of the most challenging calls to devoted Christian living found in Scripture. Some might even feel the demands are too challenging (as if God were worth less than our best). But the blessedness only comes from turning wholeheartedly to God, not in finding excuses for turning away from him.

Though the passages deserve much more consideration than we can give here, notice that God gives joy (1:14; 2:10), peace (1:79; 2:14), glory (2:32), deliverance and salvation (1:74f., 77; 2:30), and mercy (1:54). These ideas will find us again in our journey through Luke. Though given only brief note here, each is worth prolonged reflection, for here we have divine satisfaction of the deepest human needs. If these are not to be found as disciples of the Lord, they cannot really be found at all, for only God is their true source.

DISCUSSION QUESTIONS

1. Which themes discussed in this chapter feed into the discipleship idea? These themes will be developed more fully in 9:51-19:27.

2. Compare Luke 1 and 2 with Matthew 1 and 2. What is the significance of the different ways these two gospels present the birth and infancy narratives?

3. Read the poetry in these chapters apart from the rest of the text; then do the same with the prose. What do you learn by comparing the two types of literature?

4. Why do you think only Luke records the event about Jesus at age 12?

14

5. Given the material in these chapters, do you think Luke is placing greater stress on the *humanity* of Jesus, or on his *divinity*?

6. If we take the picture of Jesus in Luke 1 and 2 as a model, what do we learn about the nature of discipleship?

CHAPTER 3
■ Luke 3:1-4:15

We are now ready to move into Luke 3:1-4:15. A good way to prepare for our study is to read the text carefully before going further. I find that when I re-read a text, even one I have read many times before, new ideas often pop up to bless me. I hope the same for you.

Characteristics of the Text

The first twenty verses of chapter three basically complete Luke's story of John the Baptist. We are told about the beginning of his career, which Luke sets against three backgrounds: the Roman government, the Jewish hierarchy, and the Old Testament (vv. 1-6). It is as if Luke is saying that John's preaching should touch everyone. Then we hear John preaching, calling his hearers to repent, and delivering an exciting message about the coming Messiah (vv. 7-18). John was arrested by Herod because he had the courage to apply God's demand for repentance to the specific sins of Herod and his wife, Herodias (vv. 19f.). Before this, after John had baptized "all the people," his ministry climaxed at the baptism of Jesus (3:21f.)

This story is followed by a long section giving the genealogy of Jesus, tracing it all the way back to Adam (3:23-38). In the fourth chapter, we are told of Jesus' epic struggle with the devil in the wilderness, of the victory there, and of the retreat, but not defeat, of the Enemy (4:1-13, especially v. 13).

Discipleship in this Section

The Messiah is coming, said John. His preaching was to prepare people for this dramatic and long-anticipated event. The powerful words of John make it clear that personal change was imperative for those who desired entrance into the kingdom. The themes stressed in these verses prepare us for the details about Christian discipleship given later. John's preaching conveyed a note of urgency: the tree was about to be cut down. Repentance should not be delayed (v. 9); salvation itself was at stake (3:6; and cf. 1:77). The decision to accept or reject John's message was not a light one; the person who refused John was likened to chaff, destined to be burned with unquenchable fire (3:17).

John's preaching was radical. He rejected the assumption that the Israelites would automatically enjoy the blessings of the coming messianic age. If anyone thought that being descended from Abraham guaranteed entry into the kingdom, John smashed that assumption. Though in ancient Israel one was born into the kingdom by virtue of one's ancestry, lineage no longer ruled the day. If he wished, God could make children of Abraham from rocks, but it took a changed life to make a child of the kingdom.

If John's hearers wanted forgiveness of their sins, repentance and baptism were necessary (3:3). As we make our way through Luke's material, the same call to repent and be baptized will be sounded repeatedly. In fact, the early church described in Acts ("Luke, Part 2") understood that God's forgiveness was not possible any other way. John's message, then, was a clear preparation for the call of Jesus for repentance (cf. 13:1-5), as well as preparation for the apostolic preaching (cf. Acts 2:38).

Luke emphasizes the necessity of repentance more than any other gospel. In the present text (vv. 10-14, verses found only in Luke), John makes specific application to three groups: the multitudes, the tax collectors, and the soldiers. In every case, John stresses the need for compassion toward fellow humans. Those accepting his message would willingly share with those who lacked food and adequate clothing. Tax collectors and soldiers, who had many opportunities to take advantage of others by intimidation and force, were warned against such inhuman greed. Such mistreatment must not be a part of those preparing for the kingdom. These same emphases, on compassion and against greed, are stressed over and over in the rest of the gospel (note also 1:51-53). Because they are mentioned so often, Luke may have known that his readers had particular struggles with these problems.

Baptism was also a significant part of the discipleship process. John said it was an essential preface to forgiveness. Later, in 7:29f., Jesus described those who were baptized by John as "justifying God," while those who refused John's baptism refused "the purpose of God for themselves." It is clear, from Jesus' debate with the scribes and elders in 20:1-6, that John's baptism was from heaven, not from men. It's no wonder, then, that response to it was critical. As one moves into the text of Acts, the importance of baptism in the conversion process (becoming disciples) builds neatly on the foundation laid here (see Acts 2:38; 8:12, 36-39; 10:47f., etc.). We should note, also, that John's baptism was supplanted by a baptism into Jesus' name, in which the Holy Spirit was received (Acts 19:1-7).

We can say, then, on the basis of this preparatory material in John's preaching, that the call to discipleship is a call to repentance and baptism, since these decisions lead to forgiveness and salvation.

This section of Luke also paves the way for a fuller understanding of the role of the Holy Spirit in the life of the disciples. Verse sixteen of chapter three indicates that followers of the Messiah would be baptized with the Holy Spirit. Whatever may be the significance of "baptize" in this verse (and perhaps the word has occasioned too much doctrinal strife), it is clear that when the "mightier" one would come, the Spirit would come on all his followers. Perhaps the idea of a baptism with the Spirit implies that it would be an overwhelming experience, just as baptism in water was an overwhelming (submerging) of the candidate. As promised, the Spirit *did* come, according to the inspired witness of Peter (Acts 2:33).

Luke has much to say about the Spirit. In fact, the seventeen references in his gospel constitute a larger number than are found in any of the other three gospels. In addition, more than fifty references to the Spirit are found in Acts. For those who are curious to understand the role of the Spirit in the life of the Christian and of the church, Luke and its sequel, Acts, are an excellent place to begin. There is no better way to grasp the New Testament's teaching on the Spirit than by going directly to the text, a far better approach than buying into a view propagated by the Christian media.

I'll have more to say about the Spirit later. For now, a few observations will suffice. For one thing, Luke, in both the gospel and Acts, makes the point that all the major characters about whom he writes are Spirit-empowered. Usually he does this at a point where the character becomes prominent in the story. Notice that Luke 1:15 says John was "filled with the Spirit from his mother's womb." Presumably this endowment characterized his entire life and explains the power by which his ministry was conducted. The third and fourth chapters of Luke have four references to the Spirit in connection with Jesus (3:22; 4:1, 14, 18). In Acts, we see the Spirit coming into the lives of the Twelve (2:1-4). Stephen (Acts 6:3, 5, 10; 7:55), Philip (Acts 6:3), Barnabas (Acts 11:24), and Paul (Acts 13:9) are likewise especially blessed by God's Spirit. However, don't forget that Luke also indicates that the Spirit is God's gift to every Christian (Acts 2:38).

From these texts, we can conclude that the life of a disciple is an empowered life. Discipleship is not an unaided human effort; the God who calls also strengthens. The story is God's story, and men are his instruments. This fits with the God-centeredness noted in the events of chapters one and two. Remarkable possibilities are opened up for the

Christian who commits to be used by God's power.

Jesus received the Spirit at his baptism (Luke 3:22). At that point he began his public ministry. Luke appears to say that, when Jesus "went public" and began his work, the power to do so came from God. Next we see Jesus overcoming temptation (4:1-13). This too was done by the power of the Spirit, who led Jesus "in" the wilderness (4:1). Matthew and Mark, by contrast, say the Spirit led Jesus "into" the wilderness. Luke's wording conveys the idea of God's *continued* strength, an idea not found in the other accounts. To lead a person "in" a room says more than just leading him "into" a room. The devil's assault upon Jesus came with enormous power. But it was countered by the even greater power of the Spirit, moving Jesus to declare his fidelity to God's revelation in Scripture. Reflecting on how often I have failed in resisting temptation deepens my own appreciation for this story. We can also learn of the power by which God enables us to overcome temptation.

Next we see Jesus emerge as a teacher, and we learn that the power in his teaching came from the Spirit (4:14f.). Finally, we discover that he did the signs of the Messiah *because* the Spirit was upon him (4:18). I'm convinced that the Scripture in Isaiah 61:1, 2 read in the synagogue at Nazareth, is given at this point to show what works the one anointed with God's Spirit would do. When Jesus commented on the fulfillment of the text (vs. 21), he was claiming that he was the one of whom Isaiah had spoken. In all these texts, Jesus was pre-eminently empowered by God's Spirit. So it would be with his followers; Acts teaches us that the life of the church is a life lived and conducted by the same power.

Let me make one more point before moving to the next chapter. Later I'll speak about the way Luke presents Jesus, to whom men are called to be disciples. In view of that, we should note that Jesus is announced at his baptism (3:22) as the "beloved Son" with whom God is pleased. This word from heaven also suggests that Jesus fulfills Isaiah's beautiful picture of the Servant of God (Isa. 42:1; 52:13-53:12).

21

Jesus is also the one who resists every temptation of the devil (4:1-13) and is a teacher who is glorified by all (4:14f.). Careful reflection on this picture of Jesus should at least provoke serious consideration of him and create a willingness to ponder the possibility of following such a remarkable person. The call to discipleship is a call to follow Jesus and become like him.

DISCUSSION QUESTIONS

1. If you were an orthodox Jew listening to John the Baptist, how would you react to what he said? Shock? Surprise? Agreement?

2. What images did John use in his preaching, and what was their significance?

3. What unique things does Luke mention about John's teaching on repentance? Can you think of similar emphases elsewhere in the gospel?

4. Were John's converts forgiven, absolutely and finally? Justify your answer.

5. React to this statement: the "baptism" of the Spirit was just a way of describing the overwhelming arrival of the Spirit, like the submerging in water of baptism.

6. Compare what Luke tells us about the Holy Spirit and Jesus in 3:22-4:21 with similar material in Matthew and Mark. What is Luke telling us?

CHAPTER 4
■ Luke 4:16-6:11

Remember that the heart of our study is the central section of Luke (9:51-19:27). However, we can recognize that Luke skillfully prepares us for these chapters in the preceding material. It would be a shame if we came to the central section without being led through chapters 1:1-9:50. Jesus' Galilean ministry is described in 4:16-9:50. It is usual to divide this longer section into three parts, the first of which (4:16-6:11) occupies us in this chapter. Later we will look at the second (6:12-8:56) and the third (9:1-10) sections.

Before we plunge into Galilee, let me remind you of two things stressed before. First, remember that carefully reading the passages in Luke before proceeding with this chapter can make this study richer. Second, remember that Luke 6:40 is a key to understanding discipleship. We learned from that text that the goal of a disciple is to be like the master. As we look at Jesus though Luke's eyes in the rest of this chapter (and throughout the gospel), we should always do it while thinking of our own lives. To the extent it is possible, how can we become like him?

Contents of the Section

In these chapters, Jesus leaves the obscurity of Nazareth and becomes a public figure. We have been introduced to his teaching in 4:14f. Now, in 4:16-30, a passage that bears great significance for the entire gospel, Jesus appears at the synagogue in his hometown of Nazareth. Some amazing events take place there. Then, as he leaves Nazareth, we follow him to Capernaum. There, his teaching astounds the people by its authority (4:31f.). In Capernaum, he also confronts and casts out a demon from an unfortunate man (4:33-37). He heals Simon's mother-in-law of a fever (4:38f.) as well as healing many more, including other demoniacs (4:40f.). The next day, having sought solitude in a lonely place, he is followed by his admirers, providing an occasion for Jesus to make a significant statement about his work (4:42-44).

Chapter 5 finds Jesus by the sea of Genessaret (Galilee), where Simon Peter, James, and John are called from their work as fishermen to follow him (vv. 1-11). After calling these disciples, Jesus heals a leper in "one of the cities" (5:12-16). Then, to the amazement of the people, he not only heals a paralytic, but cleanses him of his sins (5:17-26). This event is followed by the call of another follower, Levi, the tax collector (5:27f.). Subsequently, Levi made a great feast for Jesus to which his friends, also tax collectors, were invited. The religious leaders criticized Jesus for being in such company. His response indicated his mission was to be with such people and call them back to God (5:29-32). Jesus spoke further about his work and others' response to it in stories about a wedding (5:33-35), garments (5:36), wineskins (5:37f.), and the contrast of old and new wine (5:39).

The section ends in 6:1-11 with two controversies in which Jesus and the Pharisees confront each other with regard to the true significance of the Sabbath.

Discipleship

These verses have much to say about discipleship. First, let's look again at the way in which they present Jesus, since discipleship is a call to be like the teacher. Second, we want to examine how people reacted to him, for the reactions of others invite us to inquire into our own reactions to him. And third, let's discuss some matters from the early days of his ministry which begin to define discipleship for us.

Consider the way Jesus is shown. I want to use 4:16-30

as a point of departure. This is a crucial passage in the gospel, for it presents concepts that Luke will develop in the rest of the book. It is, in effect, Luke's thesis for what he will say later. Luke, by means of the quotation from Isaiah 61:1 (v. 18) continues his emphasis on Jesus as the one empowered by the Spirit. Remember that we previously noted the Spirit coming on Jesus at his baptism (3:22), empowering him in his resistance to temptation (4:1) and empowering his preaching (4:14). Jesus applied the quotation from Isaiah to himself by his comment about the Scripture being fulfilled (v. 21). Thus he identified himself as the one who would preach good news to the poor, give sight to the blind, set at liberty the oppressed, and proclaim the acceptable year of the Lord (vv. 18). We can well see this list as presenting Jesus' ministry agenda. These services characterize Jesus throughout the gospel. His work would bring enormous blessing, especially to the afflicted and needy.

The following parts of this section of Luke stress the authority of Jesus. These references show how powerfully he came on the scene. At Capernaum, the people were amazed because of the authority with which he taught (4:32). He amazed these same people by his authority to invade the demonic world and control the wicked powers there (4:33-37, 41). To a people living in terror of evil spiritual powers, this authority was awe-inspiring. He had authority to overpower disease and bodily ailments and to bring wholeness. He cured the fever of Simon's mother-in-law (which means he cured the condition causing the fever) in 4:38. We also see him curing leprosy (5:12-16) and paralysis (5:17-26), as well as various other diseases (4:40). He even possessed the authority to control nature (5:1-11). He described himself as lord of the Sabbath (6:5). He had authority over religious tradition (5:33-38). He had authority to "compel" people to follow him (5:11, 28). Perhaps, most impressively and significantly of all, he even had authority to forgive sin (5:20).

In these stories, Luke brings Jesus before his readers so

they can consider him and make a decision about whether or not his call to "follow" should be accepted or rejected. What would it mean to follow a person like Jesus? What would it mean to refuse a person with such great power?

This picture of Jesus is further developed by three statements indicating his sense of mission. These indications of his intents and goals invite the reader to consider the implications for one who would be like the teacher. First, when Jesus went, at daybreak, to a lonely place, and was found there by the people, he told them, "I must preach the good news of the kingdom of God to the other cities also; for I was sent for this purpose" (4:43). They wished him to stay, but he felt the imperative urge to let the kingdom word be spread abroad, rather than be restricted to one location.

Second, we are told that Simon, James, and John were first afraid of Jesus and his power. But he turned aside their fear and called them to follow him. This call challenged them to the task of catching men (5:10). Not only does this episode tell us of Jesus' vision of his task, but it gives the reader a preliminary impression of an important part of discipleship—catching men.

Jesus' third statement about his mission is in 5:32: "I have not come to call the righteous, but sinners to repentance." Jesus' response to the criticism that he was associating with the wrong people, implied God's love, even for sinners, and God's willingness to go searching for such people. His call also points forward to another important dimension of the goal of discipleship.

One more facet of Luke's presentation deserves consideration. As part of a larger scheme to show Jesus as the perfect man, Luke emphasizes, throughout the gospel, Jesus' prayer life. Previously Luke showed us Jesus praying at his baptism, before the descent of the dove and the heavenly announcement (3:21f.) The text in this section is 5:16. After healing a leper, Jesus "withdrew to the wilderness and prayed." This passage, like the baptism text, is found only in Luke's gospel. What does it mean that Jesus excused himself from all the people about him for this solitary retreat? In other words, at that moment, was being alone with God more important than being with the multitudes? Does it mean that Jesus periodically retired for prayer, so that his life was punctuated by these times of intense relationship with God (this is the sense of the NRSV translation)? Both interpretations of the original language are possible. In either event, the disciple learns something about the importance of the life of prayer. When we arrive at Luke 11:1-13, we will see how it develops this concept more fully.

These words of Luke should encourage us to look at our own lives. How do we react to this figure he brings before our eyes? To enhance this personal consideration, Luke gives us a colorful panorama of reactions by Jesus' contemporaries. These reactions can be seen in miniature in 4:16-30. Notice, in verse 22, that the people spoke well of him and wondered at his gracious words; but, shortly, their attitude changed, perhaps provoked by his words in verses 23-27, and they were "filled with wrath." They even tried to destroy Jesus, but he was able to escape from their anger (v. 30).

These two perspectives, the positive and the negative, dance around one another throughout the gospel, until the climactic struggles of the end chapters. In addition to 4:16-30, reactions to Jesus are noted frequently in other texts in this section. Not only do they also reflect both acceptance and rejection, but they also indicate other nuances of response to him. Positively, people were astonished (4:13), and amazed (4:36), and they glorified God because of his activity (5:26). Great numbers of people gathered to him when they heard of his deeds. Some received specific calls and decided to follow him (5:11, 28).

On the negative side, there were those who murmured against him because of his association with tax collectors and sinners (5:30). Some tried to find some fault for which he could be criticized (6:2, 7). Finally, we are told his opponents were filled with fury at him and "discussed with one another what they might do with Jesus" (6:11).

These reactions continue throughout the gospel. I won't mention them all but, as you read, you might note them and reflect on the way they encourage the reader to ask, "How would I have reacted to him had I been there?" We know, too, that the decision to follow was not made by everyone. Some found Jesus so threatening and unpleasant they were determined to eliminate him. Therefore we are given the hint that followers of Jesus may face the same kind of opposition he faced, perhaps leading even to martyrdom.

Finally, we want to look at Jesus' followers themselves. Notice first the way Luke describes the decision of Simon and his friends (5:11) and the decision of Levi (5:28). In both cases, he says they "left everything" and "followed him." These passages might escape our attention, except that in both cases the expression "left everything" is found in Luke, but not in the parallel texts in Matthew and Mark. The uniqueness of these words, and their repetition in two different cases, suggests to us that discipleship would involve the willingness to renounce any other thing for the sake of Jesus. "Leaving everything" is a clue in examining the rest of the gospel, we will discover that this is exactly the point Luke makes in other passages. For now, a glance at 14:25-33 will confirm this conclusion. There, the call is to place Jesus and the kingdom above family, possessions, and even above life itself.

Next, we discover in 5:30 Luke using the word "disciples" for the first time in the gospel. The fact the disciples were the butt of criticism for associating with "sinners" may imply they already showed a broader concern for humanity than did their critics. The text may be saying that they were willing to break tradition on the basis of Jesus' authority (vv. 30-39).

To summarize, this chapter has spoken about Luke's presentation of Jesus with the intention of encouraging the reader to give him serious consideration. We have noticed the way people reacted to him, and we have looked in particular at the way Luke begins to show us the qualities of discipleship (willingness to renounce all for him, concern for sinners) as reflected in Jesus' first followers.

One thing we have not learned from this section, which began by showing Jesus as a teacher, was the extended content of what he taught. His lessons await us in the next section, with the Sermon on the Plain (6:20-49) and the section on hearing (8:4-21).

DISCUSSION QUESTIONS

1. Why does Luke give more detail than the other gospels in the story of the rejection at Nazareth? Why does he place it at the very first of Jesus' ministry, rather than later, as in the other gospels?

2. Comment on this statement: Gospel writers were not always strictly concerned with chronology; thus, they moved stories around to suit their purposes.

3. If you were to select a public place (for example, an airline terminal) and ask people at random what they thought of Jesus, what answers do you think you would hear?

4. Though Jesus only did good, there were those who disliked him intensely. Why? Would you?

5. In Jesus' Sabbath controversies (6:1-11), was Jesus changing the Sabbath law, or deepening it?

6. Do the comments in this chapter about Simon and Levi—who left everything to follow Jesus—overstate the case, or is Luke making a point here and throughout the gospel about the total call to follow Jesus?

CHAPTER 5
■ Luke 6:12-8:56

In this chapter, we are going to discuss the second section of Jesus' Galilean ministry. These materials, like the preceding, will continue to unfold the person of Jesus for the reader. But there will be a shift in emphasis, so that more will be said about his teaching, about his followers, and about what following him would involve.

Contents

Please follow in your Bible as we survey these chapters. After an all-night prayer, Jesus called his disciples and from them selected twelve as apostles (6:12-16). Then, as people swarmed to him, he taught and healed (6:17-19). Against the background of the gathering of the crowds Luke gives us the first major block of Jesus' teaching in the gospel— the Sermon on the Plain (6:20-49).

Then we are told Jesus entered Capernaum, where he healed the slave of a centurion (remotely, as it were—7:1-10). Shortly afterward, near the village of Nain, he amazed the onlookers by raising a widow's only son from the dead (7:11-17).

Followers of John came to Jesus, asking if Jesus was "he who is to come." In Jesus' response he pointed to the works he had done, formerly and at that very time, as testimony to his identity (7:18-23). Then he spoke to the crowds about John, using the occasion to speak also of the greatness of the kingdom of God and of the blessing of being in it. Jesus measured response to that kingdom in terms of whether people had or had not accepted John's baptism (7:29f.). Then, using a saying about children's games, Jesus chastened those who closed their minds to an acceptance of God's messengers, whether John or Jesus (7:31-35).

Chapter seven closes with the beautiful story of the sinful woman in the house of Simon the Pharisee. She came to Jesus seeking new life and found it, much to the chagrin of Jesus' critics (7:36-50).

Chapter eight begins with a summary statement about Jesus' ministry, with special mention of certain faithful women who followed and supported him (vv. 1-3). The texts which follow center on the importance of hearing and obeying God's word (parable of the sower—8:4-8; explanation of the parable—8:9-15; sayings about light—8:16-18; and Jesus' true mother and brothers—8:19-21).

Four miracles conclude this section. They are the stilling of the storm (8:22-25); the healing of the Gerasene demoniac (8:26-39); the healing of the woman with the hemorrhage (8:42b-48); and the raising of Jairus' daughter (8:40-42a, 49-56).

Teachings on Discipleship

In the previous chapter we discussed the way Luke presents Jesus to his readers, so they could consider whether he was a person they would want to follow. The present section continues the depiction of Jesus, though to a lesser extent. More emphasis is shifted to those who would be his disciples.

However, in Luke's description we do see a continuation of the emphasis on Jesus as a man of prayer (cf. 3:21f.; 5:16). In fact we are told in 6:12 that he prayed all night—the only such reference in the gospels. This certainly would suggest to his followers the importance of such communion with God. 7:18-23 describes certain good works of Jesus and shows how he was willing for them to identify him to John and to John's disciples (cf. 4:18f.). Since disciples of Jesus strive to be like Jesus (6:40), these texts indicate that a life of discipleship will be a life of prayer and good works.

By this point in Luke's story Jesus had attracted a great crowd of disciples (6:17, and cf. 5:1). However, this reference to "a great multitude of people" indicates that though many came, not all who came to Jesus had an interest in being his followers. Some of them had other motives. This contrast suggests that a disciple is not merely a hanger-on or one who is in the company of a teacher. To have been in the same town with Jesus, or even to have heard his sermons, did not necessarily qualify one for entrance into the kingdom (cf. 13:26f.).

It has been convincingly argued that this section of Luke could be considered the training of the disciples, especially of the apostles, based on the observation that the section begins with the selection of the Twelve (6:12-16). (Further training will be found in the central section, 9:51-19:27.) The next main section begins with the sending out of the same group in extension of Jesus' ministry (9:1-6). This suggests the intervening material, between the choosing and the sending, describes how Jesus prepared them for their work.

If we look at 6:12-8:56 in this way, several points come to our attention, all of which can teach us about our discipleship. First, disciples are people whose hearts are open to hear and learn the Lord's teaching, a point made most convincingly in 8:4-21. The parable of the sower (8:4-15) depicts the way different people attend to the preaching of God's word. Some just barely hear, with little interest, before the devil comes and takes the word from their hearts. Others hear and apparently prosper, but do not have the depth of conviction to enable them to withstand temptations. Still others make an initial response, but surrender their commitment under the pressure of "cares and riches and pleasures of life." But true disciples hear, hold the word fast in honest and good hearts, and bear fruit with patience.

Immediately following the explanation of the parable of the sower, Jesus spoke of the gospel as a secret thing that would ultimately become manifest (8:16-18). Those who would be Jesus' followers should take heed how they hear, in order that they might be blessed in richer and fuller ways.

In verses 19-21, Jesus' mother and brothers could not gain access to Jesus because of the crowds around him. When told of this, he used the occasion to teach the people that "my mother and my brothers are those who hear the word of God and do it." The community formed by hearing and obedience was so important that it even transcended blood ties.

In addition to these references, Jesus taught a strong lesson in 7:31-35 about the necessity of honest hearing in order to achieve genuine discipleship. Many of the people had rejected John because of his austere lifestyle. But when Jesus came, by contrast, with a convivial "eating and drinking" lifestyle, he was rejected as well. It was clear that the criticisms of lifestyles were only smoke screens to hide the real objections of the people. They did not want to hear any prophet of God. Their pretended reasons were a camouflage for closed-mindedness.

These passages, then, teach a most important lesson about following Jesus. It demands a spirit of submission and humility. One of the biggest barriers to genuine, committed discipleship is a refusal to practice personal honesty before God. We must not deceive ourselves into letting selfish interest deny what God says to us, yet this is easily done. Self-deception is so insidious that we often are not aware we are guilty. For this reason, disciples are called to continual inner vigilance, lest they refuse to truly "hear" the Lord.

A second point made about discipleship in this section is found in the Sermon on the Plain (6:20-49). The entire sermon deserves careful analysis, but here I will note only its central teaching. After the four beatitudes and the four woes (cf. Matt. 5:1-12) with which the sermon opens (vv. 20-26), we come to the heart of Jesus' teachings: "Love your enemies" he said. This premise, first sounded in verse 27, is developed through verse 38. Then, the rest of the sermon (vv. 39-49) is a series of encouragements to follow the teaching Jesus had given.

At this point, I encourage a careful reading of Luke 6:27-38. Notice how Jesus moves through the theme of love, restating it in various ways, illustrating it by concrete cases, contrasting it with lesser loves, and grounding it in the very love of God for men, even for those who are "ungrateful and selfish." Those who have made a serious effort to follow these teachings know how difficult a task it is, but they are encouraged by several factors. First is the knowledge that God loves his enemies. Second, there is the example of Jesus during his passion. Third, there is the help that God gives through prayer.

Notice also that love for enemies includes foregoing a harsh, critical, judgmental, and condemnatory spirit. It means that the disciple learns the arts of forgiveness and giving. It is through these perspectives that one receives forgiveness and is graced with the incredible generosity of the Father (vv. 37f.).

Love for enemies takes us to the far edge of love. If we can love them, we can love anybody. Indeed, one of the strong messages of Luke is that Christ did love everybody. We call this the "universalism" of the gospel. No one is beyond the pale of God's love. Jesus often demonstrated universalism in the gospel by extending his concern to those who were otherwise deemed outcast or unacceptable in his society. In this section of the gospel, this concern is demonstrated in two cases. Jesus healed the slave of a Roman centurion, bringing him back from the very doors of death (7:1-10). Even though this centurion, like Cornelius in Acts 10, was highly regarded by the Jewish leaders, it is still unusual that Jesus would show concern for such a man, since he was a Gentile and a Roman soldier. Even more remarkable was his commendation of the soldier for a faith surpassing even that found in Israel (7:9).

The other case showing how Jesus cared for outcasts is the story of the sinful woman in 7:36-50. The woman may have been a prostitute, but whatever she was, Jesus still offered her the opportunity for forgiveness and a new life. He was criticized, but he blessed the woman regardless. Disciples who aim to be like Jesus never exclude other humans from their loving concern, regardless of how those people are regarded by the culture in which they live.

A final point about Jesus' training of his followers concerns faith. Frequently in this section, he comments on the importance of trusting God. Such trust was not always easy, for it involved overcoming various sorts of obstacles or believing seemingly impossible things. Jesus' own surpassing trust in God is obvious from his all-night prayer in 6:12. The centurion, just mentioned, had such confidence in Jesus he believed that his servant could be healed with a word. No touch, no contact, not even any physical presence was necessary. Then Jesus said, "Not even in Israel have I found such faith" (7:9). What person, hearing these words, could forget them or their point?

The sinful woman in Simon's house (7:36-50), so moved by the chance for a new beginning, had such confidence in Jesus she was willing to come to him for help, though it meant braving the anger and biting criticism of the Pharisees. In the end of the story, Jesus told her she was saved because of her faith, and he bade her "go in peace" (v. 50). In these words he spoke of the power of trust in God exemplified by this woman, as well as delivered a stinging blow to those of a shrunken perspective who could only criticize.

Finally, the eighth chapter ends with four miracle stories. In them we find some powerful words about faith. When the raging storm at sea nearly capsized the boat in which Jesus and his disciples rode and when he stilled the storm, he rebuked his followers for their lack of faith. "Trust me," he seemed to be saying, "even in the direst of emergencies. Even in the face of the threat of death" (8:22-25).

When the woman with a hemorrhage touched his garment amidst a throng of people and then beat a timid retreat, Jesus called her back to their attention. He then complimented her faith. It was because she trusted in God's power that the touch healed her. Even her hidden faith was powerful (8:42b-48).

Finally, when Jesus arrived at the home of the distraught Jairus, it was to hear the sad news that the man's twelve-year-old daughter had died while Jesus struggled through the crowds to reach the house. Healing was one thing, but dealing with a corpse was something else. The people assumed there was no need for Jesus once death had invaded. But the Lord called for Jairus to have faith: "Only believe, and she shall be made well." Could faith even go so far that it would grant that the dead could come back to life? The mighty power of God moved into the still body, resuscitating the child and restoring her to her parents. How could the disciples ever forget the lesson taught about faith in this context?

The importance of open-minded hearing, love for all men, and complete faith in God—these truths were impressed on the minds of the apostles and of any who would hear. Jesus will have much more to say on these subjects, especially the last two, as the gospel story proceeds.

DISCUSSION QUESTIONS

1. Can you imagine what an entire night of prayer might have involved? Can you identify at all with such an experience?

2. How can we have a significant prayer life that we don't treat as a duty, or as a thing that "must be done" to be right with God?

3. Are we completely honest in our relation to God? How do bias and selfish interests keep us from this honesty?

4. We hear many voices in our culture today. What are some of them? How do we decide which to hear and which to ignore?

5. We are to love our enemies, but this command some-times seems impossible. Can you give examples? How can we solve this spiritual problem?

6. Does the language of Luke 6:37 forbid making any kind of evaluation of another person? What about an employment recommendation, or a teacher giving a grade? Discuss.

7. Just what is faith? What were those in the text (17:5) expecting to receive?

CHAPTER 6

■ Luke 9:1-50

This section records the last section of Jesus' Galilean ministry. Many of the themes noted in the previous sections come together here. The story comes to a climactic point when the disciples identify Jesus as Messiah. Upon that basis, Jesus begins to say some new things. In all this, the disciples play a prominent role.

Characteristics of the Section

Jesus called the apostles together and sent them out, with power, to preach the kingdom of God and to heal (9:1-6). Herod the tetrarch, hearing of these things, wondered just who Jesus was and sought to see him (9:7-9). When the apostles returned, Jesus took them aside to a lonely place. However, when the crowds followed them, he miraculously fed five thousand people (9:10-17). It is at this point in the narrative that Luke tells us that Jesus' disciples, for the first time, confessed him as the Messiah (9:18-20). Jesus commanded them to tell no one of their discovery (9:21), spoke of the suffering he would have to endure (9:22), and indicated the dedicated lifestyle demanded of those who would follow him (9:23-27).

These significant events were followed by the transfiguration (28-36), the healing of a demoniac by Jesus, (which countered the failure by his disciples to heal, 9:37-43a), a further passion saying (9:43b-45), a debate about greatness (9:46-48), and the story of the "strange exorcist" (9:49f.).

Discipleship in the Section

Several matters in these verses invite attention as we continue considering how Luke presents the challenge to discipleship. First, we will notice the expansion of Jesus' work by the apostles (9:1-6). Second, we will discuss the "great confession" of Jesus as the Christ, and the following words from Jesus. Finally, we will survey some surprising evidence about discipleship "failures," which will show us the necessity for the teaching of Jesus that follows in 9:51-19:27.

Jesus sent out the apostles whom he had chosen (6:12-16) to teach and heal, as he had done himself. Now it is clear why Jesus was choosing and calling followers (5:1-11, 27f.; 6:12-16). It also indicates that Jesus intended his work to be carried on by his followers. This theme becomes increasingly important through the gospel and is central in Acts.

As the twelve whom Jesus prepared went on this mission, they were to trust God to provide their needs. That God *could* provide had been previously demonstrated by the great catch of fish when Simon was called (5:1-11). These, and other indications in the gospel, show that God *would* see to it that their necessities would be supplied.

We do not know what the disciples had thought previously about the identity of Jesus. However, by the time Jesus put the question to them in 9:20, they had come to recognize that he was the Christ, or king, promised by God for his people. Notice how Luke prepares the reader for this high point of recognition by the previous question from Herod about the identity of Jesus in 9:7-9. Both texts indicate how eagerly people were discussing the identity of this teacher who had come among them. With this recognition by the disciples, we might expect some significant developments in the gospel story—and we won't be disappointed.

For one thing, the confession was confirmed and amplified by the following story of the transfiguration (vv.

40

28-36). Jesus, in his glory, was identified by the heavenly voice as the one whom men should hear. In addition to validating his Messiahship to Peter, James, and John, it implied there was even more to be known about him.

After the confession, Jesus shocked his disciples by speaking of his suffering (v. 22, also vv. 31, 44). Suffering would be the last thing one might expect to happen to a king. In a sense, Jesus' statement was "unchristlike," if we interpret "christlikeness" in terms of the popular conception of the Messiah. But there it was. If the king was to suffer, and disciples were to strive to be like him, what might be their fate?

It was appropriate then that Jesus, for the first time in the gospel, spoke in strong terms about the seriousness of discipleship (vv. 23-26 and in chapter 8). Self-denial, cross bearing, even the willingness to lose one's life for Jesus' sake—these are all staggering statements. They have become so time-worn much of their impact has been lost, but they need to become the subject of serious thought and lingering self-examination on the part of contemporary followers of Jesus. What thinking Christian would put himself or herself in a situation where the Lord himself would be forced to say, "I am ashamed of you"? Yet that was the very matter at stake (v. 25). No wonder Jesus indicated that even if one should gain the entire world, the payoff would be an empty gain if, in such a victory, one's relation to God were forfeited.

Let us get the picture, then, of the very people who heard Jesus say these words. They could recall the place, the time, the surroundings, all the details of the scene. If anyone should have received the full impact of these words, it should have been the immediate followers of Jesus—his disciples and apostles. Yet the rest of this chapter contains a great surprise—as we pursue the story of Jesus' followers through the following verses, we are amazed at their shortcomings. They did not understand, they lacked spiritual power, and they revealed, at times, a spirit as far from that of Jesus as can be imagined. Let's survey the evidence.

In the story of the transfiguration (28-36), Peter misunderstood the nature of the occasion. Consequently, he wished to build booths for Jesus, Moses, and Elijah—not the proper response to the circumstances. Luke is more specific than Matthew and Mark, adding the words "not knowing what he said" to verse 33. Peter was indicted for failure to understand. In defense of Peter, we might note that the swirl of circumstances around him may have left him confused. His intentions were probably good.

Next, Jesus came down the mountain to be met by the entreaties of a man whose demon-possessed son could not be healed by Jesus' followers (37-43a). Jesus, in casting the demon from the boy, cried out, "O faithless and perverse generation, how long am I to be with you and bear with you?" We do not know who these powerless disciples were. However, since only Peter, James, and John were at the transfiguration, it is at least possible the other nine apostles may have been the persons in question. If so, we remember that they were given healing power in 9:2. It would seem likely that the father would seek out people who had already performed exorcisms. What had happened in the interim? Could it be that their faith had wavered so that they had lost the power Jesus had bestowed? That is certainly one possible interpretation of the text, and if correct, explains a second consecutive passage in which disciples failed.

In verses 43b-45, Jesus spoke again of his suffering. (Please note that verse 31 also seems to indicate Jesus' death.) But the disciples did not understand. As if to emphasize their failure, Luke repeats the point in several ways. Again, Jesus' followers did not grasp the true nature of things, though we can certainly see how unlikely a martyred king would seem to them.

In the next paragraph (vv. 46-48), we see Jesus' disciples arguing about which of them was the greatest. It would seem that Jesus' previous teaching on love (6:26-39) would circumvent such a debate, but it didn't.

Consequently Jesus, illustrating his point by calling a child to his side, taught his followers that "he who is least among you all is the one who is great." We will see that even this teaching was not enough to resolve the ego problems of the disciples (see Luke 22:24).

The last paragraph of the Galilean section of the gospel (vv. 49f.) pictures the disciples forbidding a man "who does not follow with us" from healing an unfortunate demoniac. To them, being in the right place with the right group was more important than allowing the exercise of compassion. It strikes us as completely contrary to the teaching and practice of Jesus for his followers to allow someone to continue to suffer for such a reason. No wonder Jesus corrected them with "'do not forbid him; for he that is not against you is for you."

Though it goes into the next (central) section of Luke (9:51-19:27), we should also examine 9:51-56, what may be the most extreme case of all the failures of the disciples. As Jesus began his trip to Jerusalem, he sent messengers ahead of him. On coming to a Samaritan village, their request for hospitality for Jesus and his company was refused—not surprising, since Jesus was traveling to a rival feast in Jerusalem. What is surprising is the request of James and John: "Lord, do you want us to bid fire come down from heaven and consume them?" Perhaps they thought if the village were turned into a scorched spot on the earth, on future occasions the Samaritans would think twice about refusing courtesy. But Jesus rebuked his disciples, and we learn how completely contrary to the spirit of the Lord himself their attitude was. So much so, in fact, that it is very difficult for us to believe they could even make such a request. But they did!

As we reflect on these six episodes (going back to 9:28), we wonder how people who had been empowered by Jesus (9:1-6) and who had come to recognize his Messiahship (9:20) could demonstrate such glaring deficiencies. Even though they had not received specific instructions on all points, the Sermon on the Plain should have led to different responses than those noted. One might think Jesus had made a mistake in choosing men who seemed to be such a group of losers. How could he win worlds with such as these? As he set his face to go to Jerusalem, it is obvious that his followers would need a great deal of training if they were even to begin to fill the place he had chosen for them. Unless they could change, Jesus would lose men, not catch them.

It is against this discouraging background that we enter the central section of Luke. Since the disciples certainly needed training, it is in this coming section that this training takes place. So we turn to these chapters with more than antiquarian interest. We too are disciples, and we recognize that our training continues through life. Therefore we will want to listen keenly to what Jesus has to say, for it is a message to us also.

DISCUSSION QUESTIONS

1. How can you explain some of the "theories" about Jesus in 9:7-9?

2. Why would Jesus' disciples conclude he was the Messiah when he exhibited none of the characteristics people expected to find in the Messiah?

3. Based on what Luke has said to this point, how much do you think the disciples really understood about Jesus?

4. Luke 9:33 says Peter did not understand. What should he have understood?

5. What is the central point of the "Transfiguration" (a word not used by Luke) story? How would you have reacted to Jesus' statements about his martyrdom? Why do you think Luke omits the story of Peter's protest to Jesus' prediction of his death?

6. In view of Jesus' earlier teaching in Luke, should we expect the disciples to have understood the point Jesus made in verse 48?

7. How can you explain the attitude of James and John in 9:51-56? Compare Acts 8:14-17. What caused John to change?

CHAPTER 7
■ Introduction to the Central Section

We come now to the heart of Luke, so far as teaching about discipleship is concerned. The central section (9:51-19:27) is composed of material set against the background of Jesus' final visit to Jerusalem. This is a good place to review certain observations about this section that were made in the first chapter.

1) Luke devotes far more space to this trip than do any of the other gospels. In fact, he gives it more space than all the other gospels combined, indicating that it plays an important part in the gospel, and inviting us to look carefully at its contents.

2) The text does not seem particularly interested in giving us a day-by-day travel diary of Jesus' journey. Though we are given hints of location (note 9:52; 13:22, 31; 17:11), Place doesn't seem to be the important part of each account. What is most important is the reason for the journey, and what was done while on the way.

3) These are episodes and sayings that center on a man who is on his way to die. Luke 9:51—"he set his face to go to Jerusalem"—has an ominous sound, in view of the previous passages. Jesus had twice foretold his suffering (9:23, 44) and had spoken to Moses and Elijah about his "departure" (9:31), which would be accomplished at Jerusalem. The Greek word translated "departure" is "exodus," and it is generally granted that it also denotes Christ's coming suffering, resurrection, and ascension. The reader, thus alerted, feels a sense of apprehension as Jesus sets out on his journey.

Why was he going to be killed? Why did he walk into the trap, knowing it was there? These questions press themselves upon the thoughtful reader. The answer moves us into the very heart of the gospel.

4) Finally, we remember that the people who traveled with Jesus were hardly ready to carry on his work. Our last chapter has shown us how ill prepared they were.

In view of these factors I consider the central section to be directions for disciples. Jesus was getting his followers ready for what was to come: for his fate and for their subsequent responsibility.

What we have done is to make our way through these chapters with the discipleship theme in mind. We have asked what, if anything, each passage has to say about the topic. Virtually every text in this section addresses the theme. The discussion from this point forward will share the results of this investigation.

Contents of the Section

This part of Luke is generally divided into three sections: 9:51-13:30; 13:31-17:10; and 17:11-19:27. Efforts to analyze these sections into orderly outline form are not too successful, since the material is somewhat diverse. So, instead of following the procedure adopted earlier in this book, I intend to roam through the entire section, pursuing themes and discussing their relation to what it means to follow Jesus. Thus, I won't give section summaries as I have to this point, making it doubly important that the text be read carefully. In these next few chapters, there will be numerous textual citations. Since space forbids describing each passage in detail, readers are encouraged to examine the biblical texts for themselves.

In analyzing the central section, I have arrived at the following categories:

- The picture of Jesus, the one whom we follow
- The seriousness of discipleship

• The specifics of discipleship (Love, Faith in God—including prayer—and rival "gods," whom we must not follow, which include ego and wealth)
• The blessings of discipleship

The Jesus Whom We are Called to Follow

We have already noted how Luke brings Jesus before his readers. Chapters 4:16-6:11 focused on Jesus' authority. In 6:12-8:56 he was presented in other ways (see chapter 5). Chapter 9:1-50 showed Jesus' disciples for the first time confessing him as the Messiah. In the central part of Luke our picture is expanded.

Remember that Luke is calling his readers to decision. If they are not Christians, he asks them to consider Jesus. If they're Christians, he challenges them to look at him again. If what Luke tells his readers is true, and if the readers are willing to act on the truth, then this gospel is calling for a monumental decision in becoming Jesus' disciples.

How is Luke's picture drawn? What does he have to tell us about Jesus?

1) Jesus' mission was to seek and save the lost. In the story of Zacchaeus (19:1-10), an "outcast" who received Jesus joyfully, Jesus answered those who would criticize him by affirming his primary concern for lost persons. This episode shows a divine concern that refused to stop at any human barrier. All men are precious in God's sight, and Jesus embodied that godly care.

This story reminds us of previous statements about the mission of Jesus encountered in 4:16-6:11. For the reader of the gospel who would recognize his own "lostness," this statement by Jesus offers great hope.

Is such a man worth following?

49

2) Jesus is also seen as one with the courage to denounce his generation fearlessly. The inhabitants of Chorazin, Bethsaida, and Capernaum—cities where Jesus conducted his preaching—would face the consequences of having refused his message (10:13-15). These words, spoken on the occasion of the sending out of the seventy, were followed by the announcement, in 10:16, that rejection of them was to reject Jesus, and to reject Jesus was to reject the one who sent him! No wonder Jesus spoke as he did, for he came with the very authority of God.

Not only were the cities that rejected him denounced, Jesus also had strong language for the religious leaders (Pharisees and lawyers) whose attitudes and practices were the very opposite of God's expectations for them. Read 11:37-12:1 carefully to see how courageously Jesus spoke out against the faults of these people.

In view of such straightforward preaching, one can understand Jesus' words in 12:49-53, where he likened his ministry to a casting of fire upon the earth. Then he spoke of a baptism he was to receive, a baptism usually understood to be overwhelming suffering. To conclude this passage, Jesus spoke of division, even rending the closest familial relations, because of him. The point was not that Jesus desired such rifts, but knowing human nature he was aware that his call, either accepted or opposed, could cause the most serious conflicts imaginable. The presentation of the call to discipleship in these terms offers a staggering challenge to the reader.

The issue, said Jesus, was no light one. If people would acknowledge him before others, then he would acknowledge them before the angels. But if they denied him before others, he would deny the denier before the angels (12:8f. and cf. 9:26).

Is such a man worth following?

3) Jesus spoke of his future. We have already seen that he foretold his own death (9:23, 31, 44). As he made his way to Jerusalem, he sounded this note again (13:33; 17:25; 18:32f.). If he spoke the truth, then we know he willingly accepted such a fate. Why would he do this, and what did it mean for those who would follow him?

Though predictions of his death seemed strange, perhaps it seemed even stranger when he indicated he would be raised from the dead (9:22, 18:33). Further, he would come to earth again, which implied a period of absence from earth after his resurrection (12:40; 17:22-37; 18:8; 19:15, 27). When he came again, it would mean judgment (17:33).

Is such a man worth following?

4) Jesus presented himself as one whose message must be proclaimed. He undoubtedly spoke of what he preached, and what would be preached about him, when he said that what was covered would be revealed; the hidden would be known. Words spoken in the dark would be heard in the light. Messages whispered in private rooms would be proclaimed upon the housetops (all in 12:2f.). Later, at the triumphal entry, when the Pharisees urged Jesus to stifle the exuberant praise of his admirers, Jesus said the truth they shouted would be known even if God had to give the stones a voice to proclaim it (19:40).

Certain Pharisees urged Jesus to flee the territory ruled by Herod because that king wished to kill him. Jesus' reply indicated that he was on a mission mandated by God, which no earthly ruler could thwart until allowed to do so by God himself (13:32f.).

In these statements we see a clear statement of purpose and a recognition that the inexorable power of God would bring Jesus' work to its intended conclusion.

51

Jesus further indicated his place in God's purpose by speaking of himself as the one who brought the kingdom of God (11:20; and see 17:21). Though Satan opposed the coming of God's rule, in Jesus Satan was overmatched. Jesus would invade Satan's palace and defeat him (11:21f.).

It becomes clear that Jesus spoke often of the kingdom of God, giving form and content to that expectation sp thrilling to the Jewish people. What is unusual about Jesus' words is that the concept he presented didn't fit the physical, political kingdom idea that people expected. They could well assume he didn't know what he was saying. Yet he said it with such an air of finality that it was clear he was convinced he knew its true nature. (For passages in which Jesus spoke of the kingdom, see 10:9; 11:20-22; 12:31, 56; 13:18-20; 16:16; 17:20f.; and 19:11f.)

Is such a man worth following?

5) Perhaps the most significant statement Jesus made about himself is found in 10:22. There he not only claimed that "all things have been delivered to me by my Father," but that none would know who the Father was except "the Son and any one to whom the son chooses to reveal him." This claim to sonship, and to an intimate knowledge of God, would mark a man as deranged if it were not true. For those who would know of the Father, the statement of Jesus offered staggering possibilities.

Is such a man worth following?

Reactions to Jesus

As if to highlight the need for the reader to make a decision, Luke again indicates the spectrum of reactions to Jesus. To be sure, there were those who did not accept him for what he claimed to be. Some, to explain his wonderful works, accused him of being in league with evil forces

(11:15). Doubting critics, unwilling to accept the evidence of his words and deeds, demanded that he bring them a sign from heaven (11:16). Attempts were made to trap him into words for which he could be condemned (11:53ff.). He was criticized for his sabbath activities (13:14) and for receiving and eating with "sinners" (15:2). His words about the proper attitude toward material things brought scoffing from certain Pharisees (16:14). Once it was even reported (perhaps falsely, because when Herod met Jesus later he showed no such desire—Luke 23:6-12) that Herod wanted to kill Jesus (13:31). But on none of these occasions was Jesus successfully discredited. In fact, in more than one instance the dialogue following the negative response resulted in a highly effective rebuttal to the opposition (cf. 11:17-23; 13:17; 14:6; 15:3-32).

On the other hand, great crowds of people sought to be with Jesus and praised God because of his words and actions (12:1; 13:17; 18:43). The sick came for his merciful ministrations (17:13). One important official, forgetting his dignity, climbed up a tree to be able to see him (19:4). And, on one significant occasion, a blind man addressed him as "Son of David" (18:37). These words, acknowledging Jesus as Messiah, gave a foretaste of the great acclamation of Jesus as the Messiah at the triumphal entry (19:36-44).

It may be that all this material is too familiar to Christian readers. Consequently we're inclined to let it pass by as something we have heard many times before. Is it possible to look at these matters a different way? Could we forget the biblical story for a moment and imagine how we would react if such a person came into our world? What would we do with someone who said he would die and come back to life, who claimed to show us the very nature of God, and who told us, without hesitation, that our eternal destiny hung upon our response to his words?

We might ignore him. We might try to explain him away. But we might ask, seriously, if his claims were true, and if there were any substantial reasons for doubting them,

53

spectacular as they might be. And we could very well ask, "Is such a man worth following?"

DISCUSSION QUESTIONS

1. Why would a person, knowing death awaited, go to it deliberately? How does Luke answer this question? Be specific.

2. Summarize the contents of Luke 9:51-13:30. What ideas do you find standing out in these chapters?

3. Summarize the picture of Jesus that Luke has given us as we arrive at 9:51.

4. How can you reconcile Jesus' denunciation of the Pharisees and lawyers in 11:37-12:1 with his words in chapter 6 about loving enemies?

5. Why would someone oppose a closest blood relative because they decided to follow Jesus? Do you know of any such cases?

CHAPTER 8
■ Central Section:
The Seriousness of Discipleship

Is anything more serious than death? The fact that Jesus announced his coming death as he journeyed to Jerusalem would impart a gravity to the entire episode, even if nothing else were said. But Jesus did not travel alone; many people followed him. Among them were those to whom he would commit great responsibility—the carrying on of his mission. They, too, would have to be prepared for what might come. Perhaps, like their master, they would be called to martyrdom.

But the matter was also serious, because it was God's business. Jesus, as seen in the previous chapter, came to reveal God's nature, to proclaim his message, and to do his works. Nothing could be more important than the purposes of the God of the universe. In being a part of that plan men are called to give the utmost they have to give—to the very limit.

Thus we will find in this central section numerous contexts in which Jesus spoke in sobering tones about the seriousness of discipleship. No doubt the theme could be discovered in many more passages than those we will discuss. But for those of you who have been reading the text as we work through this study, you would do well now to read the following passages carefully: 9:23-27, 57-62; 10:13-16; 11:31f.; 12:49-53, 57-59; 13:1-3, 22-30; 14:25-33; and 17:7-10.

The Unworthy Servants

Turn first to 17:7-10. Apparently the servant in this story represents the disciple. He is in complete obligation to the master, so that when he has done all that is commanded, he is still an unworthy servant. So are we. God has given life, has given everything. There is no question of man putting God in his debt. To offer God everything is the only just and logical thing for humans to do. And this recognition adds a further dimension to the seriousness of discipleship.

No Excuses

In Luke 9:57-62 we have what might be called three job interviews between Jesus and prospective followers. It is significant that they come at the very beginning of the journey to Jerusalem, as if to set before the readers certain controlling concepts about following Jesus. To the first applicant Jesus announced that the offer to follow him wherever he went would mean giving up the assurance and comfort of home. The second was told that following him took priority over family and father, even at the time of a father's funeral. The third, by the use of an analogy from plowing, learned that absolute concentration and dedication were necessary to follow Jesus. Home and family are of enormous importance; anything that supercedes and transcends them makes a fantastic claim for allegiance.

The text just noted was not the only occasion when Jesus referred to family relations as he issued his call for a complete dedication to him. In Luke 12:51-53, speaking of persecution that would come to his followers, he noted that division would even invade households, driving apart father and son, mother and daughter, etc. We will have more to say about these matters later in this chapter.

Judgment & Rejection

In several contexts Jesus described ways in which those who rejected him and his message would bring upon themselves divine rejection. The cities in which he had done much of his preaching, Chorazin, Bethsaida, and

Capernaum, would be judged even more harshly than certain proverbially wicked cities of antiquity, because they refused the opportunity Jesus brought them (10:13-15). Such words would indicate to those in the caravan to Jerusalem the consequences of their decisions about Jesus. This was not the only occasion when Jesus condemned those who refused his preaching (cf. 11:31f.)

In Luke 12:57-59, Jesus used the illustration of two men on the way to the judge. The guilty man was admonished to make matters right with his accuser before the judgment, lest he be imprisoned. In Luke's context, it would seem the accuser was Jesus; the Master was indicating the seriousness of seeing that men were in the right relationship with him.

Luke 13:1-5, in discussing repentance, makes a pointed and inescapable application. Jesus told his hearers they weren't to concern themselves over the sins of others; unless they repented, they too would perish. They were given only these two choices—no third option was offered.

Salvation was pictured in 13:22-30 as a banquet. The entry door was narrow. Those who would not strive to enter it would find themselves excluded. Outside, they would suffer terrible agony as they unsuccessfully begged admittance. The picture Jesus painted of these "outsiders" again shows the seriousness of the matters he places before humankind.

The Classic Text

All of the references discussed bear a powerful impact. However, the classic text on discipleship may well be 14:25-33. Read this text carefully, then note how it can be outlined. In verse 25 Jesus turned to the multitudes to address them. The implication seems to be that following Jesus would no longer involve just going along with the crowd. Verses 26 and 27 indicate how important true following was, and both verses end with the statement "cannot be my disciple" (RSV). Verses 28-32 give two illustrations of the need to count the cost before engaging in a project. In the one case, failure to do so would cause great financial loss as well as profound embarrassment. In the other, the result would be a terrible defeat in battle, with a great cost in human life. The teaching was "don't be a disciple if you don't know what it involves and are not willing to pay the price." Finally, verse 33 again ends with the formula (cf. vss. 27, 28) "cannot be my disciple."

These are powerful words, and they impact us with stunning force. Many of us have no doubt heard them in sermons or classes and felt ourselves deeply moved, if not burdened with a great load of guilt because of our lack of dedication. There are two groups of people—at least—who need to take these words seriously. First, there are those who have never considered discipleship. Second, there are those whose attempt at following Jesus has been feeble, and who have never really considered what that following involved. In addition to these groups, the following remarks will address a third group: those who have been left so guilt-ridden by these words that they are completely convinced they are and always will be failures as Christians—maybe even that they have no chance of going to heaven.

There are several observations relative to this passage that move away from strict involvement with the biblical text to some important areas of application.

1. Our first priority is to be sure we get the full impact of what Jesus has said. The word "hate" in verse 26 can be troublesome if we assume that Jesus here contradicted what he said elsewhere about loving. But it is generally recognized that the term, rather than implying dark, diabolical hate, is rather the strongest of ways to indicate that not even our loved ones should come before our commitment to Christ, nor should they be allowed to deter us from it. Some have suggested that the idea would be conveyed if "love less" were substituted for "hate," though others feel that word choice weakens the power of the statement.

Notice here another reference to family. The most

significant aspects of life have to do with relationships. We define much of what we are in terms of the love we share with others. Life's greatest pains come when we lose those to whom we have been closely bonded (i.e., through death or divorce). This passage comes to have personal power for me when I insert the names of those who occupy such positions in my life. Then, when I hear the call of Jesus against such a background, I sense how great a thing he is asking.

Even more extreme than the priority of discipleship over family is the call to be willing to lose one's life (vs. 26). This is amplified by the cross-bearing statement in vs. 27 (recall 9:23). We easily affirm that we would give our lives for Christ—until we really think about what that means. Then we hesitate. And... to die on a cross! I doubt that most of us could look steadily on a crucifixion without becoming ill. In some sectors of first century society, the topic was forbidden in conversation because it was so repulsive. We need not go into detail, but to any whose meditations have dwelt on crucifixion the horror of this statement will make an imprint.

Then, in verse 33, Jesus calls for the ultimate renunciation. "Renounce all he has" might apply to physical possessions, but phrase has broader implications as well.

Absolutely *nothing* should be kept if it hinders discipleship. There is no possession, no matter how long held, how valuable, how meaningful, that should not be forfeit if the call comes for it to be given up. Not that Jesus equated poverty with piety—he didn't. But what is more important than being God's person? What would you hold onto at all costs—even if it meant denying the Lord?

These aren't comfortable words. We might wish Jesus had not spoken them. But they express the utter truth; they come from the very center of reality. If we are to be disciples, they must be accepted, pleasant or not. However, I'm convinced, contrary to immediate appearances, that these words show the way to a path where unsurpassed joy is to be found—even if the path goes past a cross.

2. In what follows, we do not want in any way to diminish what has just been said. But we do need to deal with a most distressing human problem. People who hear the words of Jesus, and know they fall short of them, can sometimes become convinced that it is impossible for them to be saved. And, since all of us do fall short, we are dealing with a difficulty that we all potentially face.

Of course, we can never earn salvation. Part of our problem is because we sometimes view Christianity as if we must earn it. Even though we may deny salvation can be merited, we still believe it. Either be totally committed or be lost: these are the options we present ourselves. But we need to recognize that Jesus is speaking in terms of the absolute and, knowing our weaknesses, he won't give up on us just because we fall short. We need to remember what Luke 9 tells us about the failures of the disciples. Jesus did not tell them they were lost unless, by some miracle, they developed a total commitment that eliminated all of their reservations and drawbacks.

After all, we would expect Jesus to speak in ideal terms. Who can imagine him saying, "Sixty percent is passing. Don't try for any more"? As one who spoke for a perfect God, who asks, because he made us, for all we are and have, we could hardly have expected him to say less. This is what God ultimately wants us to be. But in the meantime, because he loves us, he accepts what we have to give and blesses us so that we will grow more and more into the complete discipleship pictured in these verses. As C. S. Lewis, citing George MacDonald, reminds us, "God is easy to please, but hard to satisfy."

No one, except the Lord himself, has ever been totally committed to God in this life, not even the great Christians about whom the Bible speaks. Our humanity invariably gets in the way. But we must try, and in that trying recognize that God understands us and our struggles, and that he works within us to change us more and more into what he wants. Still, we must recognize what the nature of his call is, and count its cost. If we begin the Christian journey

60

thinking a lackadaisical effort is all that is asked, we begin with a serious misunderstanding of the nature of discipleship.

3. Since these verses are so powerful, they are sometimes used in a manipulative way. Sincere and zealous people occasionally abuse this text because they are intensely concerned to enlist involvement in whatever Christian project has captured their interest. As I explain what I mean, please remember that we know we must be concerned about missions, or evangelism, or plans for church work. It is not against the things in themselves that I am protesting; it is rather against a misappropriation of Jesus' words, even in a good cause.

Imagine two railroad cars, separate for the time, but able to be joined together. One of the cars is our text, Luke 14:25-33. The other is whatever Christian project is currently being advocated. It may be involvement in a particular mission field. It may be a specialized method of doing evangelism. It may be a congregational project. The person abusing the text will link the project to Jesus' words, just as the two railroad cars might be coupled. The assumption is that when Jesus spoke these words, the application he had in mind was the mission field, the personal evangelism plan, or the congregational project. The implication can be drawn that refusal to be involved in whatever is represented by the second railroad car brings one under the judgment of the first car—the biblical text. It is as if one is not practicing self-denial or bearing the cross if one is not involved in that particular project. This can either be a tremendous motivator or produce huge feelings of guilt. The point, though, is not the worthiness of the project; it may be quite worthwhile. The point is that the scripture has been misused, and Jesus has been made to say something which, in fact, he did not say. And we should be very careful that we do not seize the prerogative of claiming to speak for the Lord.

We also need to beware that we don't use this text to manipulate ourselves into situations that may not be right for us. I have often heard Christians, usually young people, who read passages like this and say, "I don't feel I can have the kind of commitment Jesus asks of me unless I go live in the ghetto" (or whatever project may have captured their attention). It is just as possible to misapply a text to ourselves as to have others misapply it for us. The feelings of guilt can be as great in one case as the other. It is not unknown for people, acting impulsively and under the pressure of a false interpretation of scripture, to make serious mistakes about the specific directions their lives should take.

About what, then, was Jesus speaking when he uttered these words? I believe the answer, so far as Luke's gospel is concerned, is found in the rest of the central section, and later chapters will discuss it in more detail. But for now we will just mention that he speaks of such supreme sacrifice being paid in order to live a life that loves as God loves— to live a life which will be characterized by absolute trust in God (not falling down before the idols of ego or wealth). Perhaps because so much has been heard about love and faith we may feel these challenges are not that great. If so, we are mistaken. To live such a life—genuinely—is all any of us can handle, and more.

4. As a corollary we must remember that Jesus is not speaking of renunciation for its own sake. We are not to be like the monk who nightly goes into his cell and flagellates himself, to mortify the flesh. Renunciation is only meaningful if it is *for* something, in some greater service. We should remember the words of Paul in Colossians 2:21-23; severity to the flesh is empty if not accompanied by true adherence to Christ.

5. These words may sound too strong. But people do look for a challenge so important it calls them to give everything they have. The fact of the matter is that we have been created for such commitment, and not to attempt it is to malfunction as persons, to fail to strive to become what God has made us to be.

A Final Word

We all need to read and re-read Luke 14:25-33. We cannot afford to become jaded. No matter how long we have been Christians, no matter how well educated we are, no matter how involved we have been in church, we all need to hear this clear call again. Over and over we must place ourselves before the challenge, and respond to it as best we can. If we do so, the faith becomes continually more exciting. Many blessings will come to us, one of the greatest of which is that we will become more like our Master each day. And to become like him, remember, is the heart of being a disciple (Luke 6:40).

DISCUSSION QUESTIONS

1. How would you react to those who argue one can be saved only if one practices "total commitment"?

2. Summarize Luke 13:31-17:10. What ideas stand out?

3. How many texts in Luke 9:51-19:27 deal with discipleship and family?

4. Does the narrow door in 13:22-30 indicate that God only wants to save a few people, or that only a few people will want to be saved? Discuss.

5. Does 14:25-33 apply to us today, or was it only for the special case of those following a man on his way to die?

6. Is it appropriate to apply "cross bearing" texts to difficult situations in life, such as a bad marriage, caring for a dependant loved one, or prolonged illness?

7. Does "cross bearing" indicate we are not genuine Christians if our faith doesn't cause us pain? How does

cross bearing work together with the idea of Christian joy?

8. Give examples of people who use 14:25-33 as a "guilt motivator" to get others to support their favorite cause(s).

CHAPTER 9
■ Specifics of Discipleship: Love

In the preceding chapters we have discussed the way Jesus is pictured in Luke's central section, as well as his statements about the seriousness of discipleship. But following Jesus must have some content. If I decide to be a disciple, what do I do? How do I live? What are my attitudes, my priorities? In this chapter we will begin to look at some of the references that answer this question.

Jesus, the Demonstration of Love

In Luke, as throughout the New Testament, the practice of love is a cornerstone of the disciple's life. Remember that Jesus is the one who reveals the Father (Lk. 10:22). In that revelation he shows us God as the one who loves all people, even the ungrateful and the selfish (Lk. 6:35). It is because of this divine love that disciples, who have received love, are called to extend it to others.

Jesus was the perfect human demonstration of this love. Remember, a disciple "when he is fully taught, will be like his teacher" (6:40). It could well be argued that everything that Jesus did and said was motivated by love. For example, many of the scenes within the gospel show Jesus in the presence of persons whose bodies were not whole. Surely among them were a number whose appearance and afflictions made them repulsive. But Jesus stayed in their midst, and by God's power made them well. His love was shown, not only by his association with them, but by his healing them, and by the promise implied in those healings that God intended to bless them even more fully.

Luke delights to picture the concern of Jesus for the

societal outcasts of his day. He was found in company with tax gatherers and sinners (how broad a spectrum this word covers). He had an interest in bringing God's blessing to women—a group held in little regard in that culture. On the cross he promised paradise to a man whose crime had brought upon him the death penalty (23:43). It is apparent that Jesus cast the net of God's love so wide that none were beyond its reach.

Jesus loved his followers. He bore with them patiently during all the trying days he was training them as disciples. Many times he encouraged them to perseverance. As a case in point, we can note the prayer in Gethsemane (22:40-46). There Jesus agonized in ways beyond our understanding. But both before and after his anguished prayer, he showed his love for his followers by urging them to pray, that they might escape their own temptation (vss. 40, 46).

Jesus came to offer the forgiveness of God to undeserving humans. Never did he withhold the offer of cleansing. Even the most depraved person, willing to heed his call, could know the purification God alone could give—witness a sinful woman (7:36-50), a chief tax collector (19:1-10), and a criminal (23:43). Nor are these the only cases. But they shine forth with the love of Jesus beamed onto darkened lives. Jesus proclaimed this message of love, and he sent his followers out to spread the news even more broadly (9:1-6; 10:1-12).

He cared for the poor. Luke's gospel is, in fact, deeply concerned to tell us of such people. There was Lazarus (16:19-31), apparently a righteous man despite his misfortunes. Further, on at least two occasions, Jesus instructed followers (or a would-be follower) to sell all they had and give to the poor (12:33; 18:22).

There is another way Jesus showed love, which is less appreciated by modern people. We tend to "live and let live." What others do is their own business, and we certainly don't confront them if they're doing wrong. But Jesus frequently confronted people who were wrong. Those who were curious about the relation between tragedy and sin were told, in 13:1-5, that they themselves needed to repent (or perish!). A man who asked Jesus to decide a matter of an inheritance was warned to beware of covetousness himself (12:14). People who were curious about the number who would be saved were told, "Strive to enter by the narrow door; for many, I tell you, will seek to enter and will not be able" (13:23). In these and other instances, Jesus recognized people were on a wrong and destructive path. He was unwilling to let them continue in their way; he loved them too much. So he took a risk and confronted them. Though confrontation can be abused by some who use it as a way to feed their own self-righteousness, still disciples who love as Jesus did will find themselves in circumstances where they too must speak out of love for those who are headed for damnation.

None of these exhibitions of love was the greatest instance in Jesus' life. That was to come on a cross, and we still do not fully grasp its magnificence.

The Teaching

During his Galilean ministry, prior to the trip to Jerusalem, Jesus sounded the call to love. The Sermon on the Plain (6:20-49) centered in the concept of love for the enemy. In that sermon, Jesus taught that such love had its source in the very nature of God (vs. 35). Thus, what the Lord taught about love was applying to specific cases the very nature of God.

This means that love is generated from the relation of the disciple to God. As we receive divine love, we bestow it upon others. Like divine love, our love depends upon the character of the lover, not of the beloved. It extends to all, no matter how undeserving they might be. Furthermore, it is not bestowed for selfish reasons, in the hope it might be repaid. In Luke 14:12-14, Jesus told his hearers to extend hospitality to the poor, the maimed, the lame, and the blind: "They cannot repay you," he said. So love is to be given for God's sake, not for selfish advantage. But in being offered to all people, this love must never degenerate into an easy tolerance of wrong.

In the Sermon on the Plain (6:32-34), Jesus distinguished between "natural" love and "supernatural" love. The former is given to those who are attractive and who can benefit the giver. Even sinners give this kind of love. Jesus did not prohibit it, but he indicated that his disciples were to go beyond "sinner love.". They were to love, "expecting nothing in return" (vs. 35). Those who love Jesus will love all people as he did and will not be concerned about being blessed or rewarded by those whom they have loved.

Luke 10:25-37 addresses the issue as well. A lawyer inquired of Jesus about the way to eternal life (cf. 18:18). Jesus called his attention to the law, which said to love God with all one's being (Deut. 6:5) and to love one's neighbor as one's self (Lev. 19:18). It became clear, however, that the lawyer was only willing to love his neighbor if he could define that term narrowly. Jesus responded with the well-known story of the good Samaritan. He taught that the word "neighbor" has no limits and that deeds of love should be performed for anyone in need. In fact, it is possible that the man who benefited from the kindness of the Samaritan may never have known his benefactor. Thus, any definition of love that excludes even a single person is less than what is expected of a disciple and imperils discovery of the way to eternal life.

There is another issue in the story of the Good Samaritan. What does it mean to love God? How is it done? If we think about it, we can see that love for God is largely shown by the way one's fellows are treated. Thus, a refusal to love others is really a refusal to love God. "Feelings" of love for God—imagined or real—do not change this fact.

Another dimension of Jesus' teaching concerned love for the lost. Indeed, this is the great truth behind the incarnation itself. The classic texts are found in the entire fifteenth chapter of the gospel, which is a unit. It begins with criticisms of Jesus because of his association with sinners (cf. 5:30; 19:7). Jesus responded with the stories of the lost sheep (vss. 3-7) and the lost coin (vss. 8-10). Both showed great concern for that which had been lost, and both stressed the heavenly joy over one sinner who repents. Then Jesus told the magnificent story of the prodigal son (vss. 11-37), which powerfully showed the nature of repentance and the lavishing of love upon the penitent. The theme statement, repeated in verses 24 and 32, is that the son who was dead was now alive, and who was lost was now found. These marvelous words reflected God's overwhelming concern for humans and their redemption. The latter verses (25-32), depicting the elder brother, were a way of showing Jesus' critics just what kind of people they were and how far they were from knowing the heart of the Father.

It is true that Christians have faced difficult questions in considering their relations to the lost world. But we must not forget that love for those out of fellowship with God is an absolute part of discipleship. Those who lack it have failed to discover a highly significant part of the gospel story. True evangelism is motivated by this love, rather than by attempts to set records or to earn salvation or to triumph in argumentation. People want to be loved and God wants us to love them. People don't want to be manipulated or browbeaten.

Here and there in the gospel, other texts can be found that give concrete form to the call to love. Luke 6:27-30 specifies doing good, blessing, praying, and returning good for evil. Verses 37ff. of the same chapter speak of not judging or condemning, but rather giving and forgiving. It can be argued that these four items continue the description of love found in the preceding verses. In chapter 17:1-4, love means not causing another person to sin (note the strength of Jesus' illustration), as well as rebuking, and also forgiving.

Love, however, cannot be dispensed by some code of

rules. It is an attitude, and those who understand their relationship with the Lord will not be at a loss as to how love should act. In Luke 6:31 we are given the Golden Rule, which might be considered a slogan for determining loving action. Jesus asked his followers to determine how they would care to be treated, and then to treat others the same way. Selfish people can pervert this text, but if we want to be loved with the authentic love of God, we must apply this rule and arrive at the right conclusions.

Let us never diminish, neither in thought nor in action, the significance of love. Love is the very heart of God, of Christ, and of the gospel. Here too should the very heart of the Christian dwell.

DISCUSSION QUESTIONS

1. Summarize Luke 17:11-19:27. What ideas stand out?

2. Distinguish Christian love and kindness (i.e. the idea that love could never "hurt" anyone).

3. How do you react to today's "live and let live" philosophy when you see others doing wrong in ways that are spiritually damaging?

4. How can a "rebuking" love become unchristian?

5. How does the love taught in the Sermon on the Plain differ from the common conception of love we see today?

6. Just how do we love God and men, especially if we don't have loving feelings?

CHAPTER 10
■ Specifics of Discipleship: Faith

Love is one great demand of discipleship emphasized by Jesus in Luke. Faith in the Lord and in divine power is the other. We have seen who Jesus is and what God's power can do. Are we willing to place our lives on that foundation? Were Jesus' followers willing to place their lives on that foundation?

Faith

It is not always easy to trust Christ. Consequently, humans are prone to commit their lives to other faith centers. One alternative that claims many is materialism. With this faith center, what has been created, rather than the Creator, is given first place. Another is the human ego; man makes himself his own god. Jesus had much to say about both of these. Consequently, our discussion of faith will talk about the positive side in this chapter. In the next two, it will discuss the two "rivals" for human allegiance, material things, and self.

If we think about life at all, we come to realize that so much is beyond us. We are forced to trust others, especially when we come to those areas of life we cannot handle alone. One of the greatest follies of life is not to recognize this dependence. Jesus' followers, in the years after his death and resurrection, would need great faith in God to persevere in Christ's work. Not only that, such faith would make it possible for the most remarkable things to happen through them.

What does it mean to live by faith in God? More than we can imagine, I am sure. But it does mean that we have a view of reality that sees God as the Originator, the Center, and the Sustainer. All life then takes meaning from that realization; it governs how we think and how we behave.

It also means that one believes God's promises and lives in view of them. Belief is not so difficult in good times. In bad times, it is much more of a challenge. It is also very difficult when one lives in an age where naturalistic assumptions permeate the culture and few people are willing to grant that God's promises can actually be fulfilled.

Faith means that God is obeyed, no matter how radical or even unreasonable his demands sound. He is obeyed because we know that what he has asked is best for his children. To take any other course of action is to invite self-destruction.

As we move through the texts selected from Luke, the nature of faith will be revealed in other dimensions as well.

Jesus' Previous Teaching

When Jesus spoke of faith on the way to Jerusalem, his words served to reinforce what he had said earlier. In chapter 5, we discussed several of these passages. In Luke 7:1-10 Jesus commended a Roman centurion for his trust, saying "Not even in Israel have I found such faith." This man had a powerful conviction that God's power could solve the problems of illness and death. The story said to Jesus' followers, "Do you have such faith?"

In Luke 7:50, Jesus told the sinful woman that the forgiveness she had received was related to her faith. She trusted that Jesus was able to give her a new start in life.

When Jesus stilled the storm on Galilee, during the following calm he asked his disciples, "Where is your faith?" (Lk. 8:25). Did they trust that Jesus could care for them in the face of grave danger?

A woman who had suffered with hemorrhaging for a dozen years touched Jesus' garment, was healed, and faded away into the crowd. Jesus called her from her concealment to make a point about her faith—perhaps to indicate that even a hidden faith has value. This story (Luke 8:42b-48) demonstrated once again to the disciples that God could bring wholeness. Would the disciples believe?

The greatest enemy is death. Jairus, in Luke 8:49, received the heart-crushing news that his only child, a 12-year-old daughter, had died. Jesus, in response, issued a tremendous challenge to the father: "Do not fear; only believe, and she shall be well" (vs. 50). Would Jairus believe that even death must succumb to the mighty power of God wrought as it worked through Jesus? Will the reader of the gospel believe it?

In the Central Section

The third part of Luke's central section (17:11-19:27) says a great deal about faith. It has been suggested that a theme for the section could be "Will men have sufficient faith to enter and be sustained in the kingdom of God?" The stories in the section encourage faith in view of the future actions of God (17:22-37; 18:15-17; 19:11-27). They also give us pictures of those whose faith was sufficient and of those who did not have the requisite trust in God. In the former category, we find the lepers (17:11-17), the persevering widow (18:1-8), the tax collector (18:9-14), the blind man (18:35-43), and Zacchaeus (19:1-10). In the latter are the Pharisee (18:9-14) and the rich ruler (18:18-30).

In the verses preceding this third part of the central section, Jesus' disciples asked him to "Increase our faith!" (17:5). The request was an interesting one. How should it be answered? What did they expect of Jesus? Was it possible they wanted something done for them so that through no effort of their own, faith would come into their lives? Whatever their desire, Jesus' answer sounded strange. He told them (vs. 6) that even a tiny amount of faith could uproot and move the sycamine tree (translated "mulberry" in the NIV), a tree with a root system that would make such an accomplishment quite difficult.

What did this answer mean? I think Jesus was indicating to his disciples how great a thing faith could be. There was no question about the power of God. The question was how much men would trust that power in ordering their lives. Even the slightest trust, Jesus seemed to say, could accomplish remarkable things. What, then, could happen if one had a greater measure of faith? Perhaps Jesus was doing a "selling job." Once the vision of the greatness of faith was seen, then it would be a goal toward which any necessary effort would be expended. How much faith could a person have? That would be up to the person. Knowing the power of faith, one should decide to trust God to the utmost.

Does it Really Work?

Since faith is not sight, those who want a more tangible verification will be inclined to say of the faith view, "it doesn't really work." Disciples of Jesus would themselves be tempted to take this point of view, for various reasons. Luke recognized this, and so he shows us several episodes in which the practice of faith had to overcome certain barriers.

One of these barriers was the barrier of general human experience. The critic of the faith view would argue that "things just don't happen that way. Therefore faith is senseless." Prior to Luke's central section, we see Jesus coming, finally, to the home of Jairus (8:49-56). He was there to attend to the man's grievously ill daughter. But the word came upon his arrival that she had died. Despite Jesus' words of reassurance, there were those who thought his presence no longer necessary. And when he said that the girl was not dead but only sleeping, there were those who laughed at him. She was clearly dead. But Jesus was saying that he had power over death, and that the child's father should believe that. To the joy of the father, and likely to the amazement of the skeptics, the girl was brought back from the dead. The faith view triumphed!

A similar story is told in 18:1-8. A widow, desiring a favorable verdict from a judge, could not "reasonably" expect it, because neither personal favor nor religious appeal could move the judge who neither feared God nor regarded men. But the woman's faith, demonstrated in her persistence, finally won the day for her. Again, faith triumphed over the apparently contradictory evidence of experience.

Sometimes the faith view seems invalid because of the immediate circumstances of life. Luke 17:11-19 tells of ten lepers who cried out from a distance to Jesus for mercy on their pitiful state. Jesus told them to go to the priest, who could verify their healing. The text tells us they were healed "as they went." This is significant, because it means they had to begin the trip to the priest while their bodies were still afflicted with the disease. It would have been easy for them, since they were not yet well, to think that Jesus' words meant nothing, and that the journey to the priest was not worth making. In other words, they had to begin the trip on faith, despite the contrary evidence of their still-diseased bodies. But they went—and were made well—as faith triumphed over the contrary evidence of their immediate circumstances.

Often it's hard to have faith when popular pressure attempts to force us away from it. A blind man in Jericho (18:35-43) joined his voice to those of all the others who cried out to the passing Jesus for his concern and help. I suppose his cries were part of a great babble of noise through which Jesus passed. Those in front, perhaps trying to diminish the clamor, told the blind man to be quiet. Had he been willing to yield to their pressure, he would have ceased his cries and would probably have been blind the rest of his life. But he believed that Jesus could heal him, so he ignored those who would silence him and cried out even more desperately. It was then that Jesus, hearing, called him from the crowd. When asked what he wanted, the blind man replied, "Lord, let me receive my sight." Jesus gave him his request, with the announcement "your faith has made you well." Faith was victorious over the popular pressure to the contrary.

Finally, men are sometimes moved away from the faith life-style because they accept common assumptions about the source of security. This temptation is particularly strong with regard to our material welfare. As we'll see in another chapter, the pressure to become materialistic is a strong one, often created by fear that unless we have the right "things," we cannot be assured about future security. In Luke 12:22-34, however, Jesus addressed the issue of wealth and fear, telling his disciples they should live in the faith that God, who made them, would care for them, reinforced by a series of arguments showing God would and could see to their needs. With that far greater sense of security, they would not need to become materialists; faith could then—and can today—triumph over the fearful "spirit of the age" in the matter of provision for the future.

Perseverance

In the faith life, as taught by Jesus, there was not only the question of whether God would be trusted at all, but also the issue of whether that trust would continue. Jesus was calling his disciples to a lifetime of service, and he knew it was a life that might well involve faith-challenging difficulties. Therefore he had a need to encourage his disciples to hang on for the long haul. Luke, as he wrote to those whom he knew would read his gospel, probably had the same concern. Thus there are a number of places where perseverance—the maintenance of faith through all circumstances—was taught by the Lord.

In Luke 12:35-46, Jesus told three stories to encourage constant preparedness on the part of his followers. The first (vss. 35-38) illustrated the point by referring to those who were ready when their master returned home from a wedding feast (regardless of the hour of the night). Those who were prepared would be blessed, because the master would "gird himself and have them sit at table," and he would serve them. The reference seems to be to the blessings enjoyed by those ready when the Lord returns. The second illustration (vss. 39f.) had to do with people who protected their possessions by being alert so that they would not be robbed. Like householders whose preparation allowed them to live in safety, so prepared people would be ready when the Son of Man came, even at an unexpected hour. Finally (vss. 41-46), Jesus contrasted a steward who faithfully discharged his responsibilities in his master's absence with one who did not. The former would be blessed, while the latter would be punished and put with the unfaithful. In all these cases, it is clear that no one could play a guessing game about the Lord's return. The only certain way to be ready for his appearing is to be ready always. This takes perseverance. Faith needs to be constant.

Beyond the central section, in the famous "apocalyptic discourse" of Luke 21, Jesus made the same point. This much-discussed speech, dealing with coming events (the destruction of Jerusalem; the coming of the Son of man) was not intended to be a key for some scheme of predicting the future, though it often receives such a misapplication today. It was meant to speak to disciples who would face various trials and difficulties, and to encourage them to remain true to the Lord through everything. Note that the text speaks of false Christs (vs. 8), wars (vs. 9), natural calamities (vs. 11), persecutions (vss 12-19), and the destruction of Jerusalem (vss. 20-24). Any one of these things was potentially faith-destroying. Jesus knew that! So, in his love for his followers, he warned them, and gave them numerous encouragements (vss. 8, 9, 13, 14, 19, 21, 28, and 36), so that they would be true to their commitment to him.

Prayer

Finally, the call to faith is a call to pray. Those who believe in God's power are given the privilege of calling that power into their lives, through prayer and the presence of the Holy Spirit. The classic prayer text in the New Testament is Luke 11:1-13. Read this text carefully. It has far more to say that we can possibly discuss here. But we should notice the following points.

1) Jesus made a remarkable promise that prayer would be heard and answered (vss. 9-13). Indeed, it seems that God is more eager to answer than people are to ask. It almost seems that God, through Christ, makes himself the beggar, beseeching his children to receive the blessings he would like to bestow.

2) Though the words of vss. 9f., promising an answer to those who ask, seek, and knock, are interpreted by some as an open-ended promise, they are not. Jesus was not guaranteeing his disciples that God would give them anything, provided their faith was adequate. Common sense tells us the verse couldn't really mean that, since God is not in the business of scattering million-dollar homes, fifty-thousand-dollar cars, and yachts to any disciple who asks for them. The context has told us the things for which we are to ask, the things that God wills to give us. Note that Jesus indicated the content of prayer in vss. 2-4, in the famous model prayer. When praying, one should pray in harmony with God's purposes, the prayer that guarantees divine response. This point cannot be stressed too strongly. If it is not observed, prayer is victim to human selfishness and ignorance.

3) We should pay special attention to the model prayer and its petitions. As I understand it, "hallowed be thy name" asks God to make the one who prays the sort of person whose life and conduct declare God's holiness. Prayer for the kingdom to come asks that God's rule may claim more and more lives. Thus, this petition has a strong evangelistic flavor. Prayer for daily bread recognizes the real source of material provision. Forgiveness of sins would take on special meaning with

the crucifixion and resurrection. "Lead us not into temptation" asks that God's power keep the disciple from being mastered by temptation and thus fall into the hands of Satan.

4) Note especially vs. 13, where the Holy Spirit is a promised response to prayer. I believe the Spirit is the power through which prayer is answered. Paul said (Rom. 8:26) that the Spirit helps us as we pray, and Jesus said the Spirit works in answering prayer. The entire prayer process is conducted in divine power—if we have faith.

DISCUSSION QUESTIONS

1. Compare the way faith is shown in Luke with the way we should show it today.

2. Is it possible to claim we have faith when the object of our faith is not realistic?

3. What are wrong things in which modern people place faith?

4. What do you think the request "increase our faith" expects for an answer? How would you interpret Jesus' answer?

5. Give contemporary illustrations of the barriers to faith indicated in this chapter.

6. Did Jesus teach God would give us anything we believe he can give? If he did, what would be the consequences?

CHAPTER 11
■ Specifics of Discipleship:
The Danger of Faith in 'Things'

Though most of Jesus' disciples do not seem to have been wealthy, they were still given considerable instruction about the potential corrupting influence of wealth as they traveled toward Jerusalem. Of course, human insecurity is such that anyone is in danger of becoming unduly attached to what has been created rather than to the Creator. Thus Jesus' words would have been appropriate for any group. I suspect, however, that Luke included these sayings of Jesus not only because of what the Lord told his followers, but because of a problem he knew existed among his readers. It seems possible that the Christians of Luke's day, several decades after Jesus walked the earth, struggled with the problem created by possessions or the desire for them. Some have suggested the delayed return of the Lord had altered the perspective of these early Christians so that they became too attached to this world.

Whatever the case might have been, it is clear Luke's gospel has far more to say about the subjects of wealth and poverty than any other gospel. In fact, he writes more on the topic than all the other gospels combined. Hardly a chapter goes by without some reference to the subject, and the same concerns surface in the book of Acts as well.

For our purposes, however, we will restrict ourselves mainly to the central section of the gospel. There are seven passages we should examine. Of these seven, five are in chapters 12 and 16, the two great "wealth" chapters of the gospel. Five of the passages are unique to Luke; only the second and sixth are found in the other gospels.

The Texts

LUKE 12:13-21

Jesus, asked to arbitrate a dispute between brothers about an inheritance, sensed a larger problem than the one presented to him. Consequently he refused to be a judge, but rather confronted the man who came to him: "Take heed, and beware of all covetousness; for a man's life does not consist in the abundance of his possessions" (vs. 15). Then he told the story of the rich fool. Here was a man, blessed with an overabundant harvest, who built larger storage facilities. The man then made the assumption that material possessions in such great measure ensured fulfillment of all of life's needs. However he forgot one need—the greatest of all—his need for God. Consequently when God announced his coming death, it was with the ominous message that his goods, whatever their value before, would be of no help in meeting his Maker. They would, in fact, go to someone else, and be of no benefit to their former possessor. Jesus ended the story with the saying, "So is he who lays up treasure for himself, and is not rich toward God" (vs. 21).

LUKE 12:22-34

This passage, dealing with anxiety, is common to Luke and the Sermon on the Mount (Matt. 6:19-33). We are specifically told that Jesus was addressing his disciples and the subject was anxiety (vs. 22). One reason people are materialistic is greed, but another is fear, and that latter reason is addressed here. Jesus' conclusion was that one need not worry about material needs, for they are known by God, and he is able and willing to provide for his children. Jesus gave several reasons to support his case. One built upon the recognition that God has already given us our lives and our bodies. If he has done this, which is the greater miracle, he can certainly see to it that we have food to sustain the body and clothes to cover it (vss. 22f.). This would be so much the lesser miracle that we should have no difficulty believing in it, once the greater miracle has been accepted.

A second argument was based on nature. God feeds the ravens, who do not work to provide a store of food for the future. If God does that for birds, how much more will he do it for his people (vs. 24). And God created the lovely lilies, more beautiful than the garments of Solomon, to clothe the grass, blooms that would only last until the heat of mid-summer. How much more could God's people depend on him for clothing (vss. 27f.)! Thus, the two illustrations dealt with food and clothing, the two items mentioned in connection with the first argument.

Third, Jesus pointed out that worry did not make one live longer (vss. 25f.). Length of life is in God's hands. The disciples were called to trust him for their sustenance.

Because God can be trusted, his disciples could afford to be generous in their provision for others (vs. 33). They were called to sell their possessions and give alms. They need not worry about losing their treasure, for their confidence in God had led to their possession of treasure in heaven, wealth that could not be lost by thievery or by the ravages of nature.

Jesus' concluding words in this antidote to anxiety were "For where your treasure is, there will your heart be also" (vs. 34).

LUKE 16:1-13

This text has two parts: verses 1-9 are the story of the unjust steward; verses 10-13 are a series of sayings on wealth. We do not know if both parts were spoken on the same occasion, or if Luke put them together here because of the common subject.

Verses 1-9 tell of a steward who, because of irresponsible performance of his obligations, was notified that he would be discharged. He desperately sought a way to insure his future. At last he hit upon a scheme: he would obligate his master's debtors to himself, so that he could use their gratitude as a way to provide for his future. The deed was done. When the master, who may have been a rascally sort himself, learned of it, he commended the "dishonest steward" for his prudence. The point was that even a person with a shady value system had enough wisdom to manipulate wealth to his advantage. In concluding the story (this text is difficult, but the general meaning is clear), Jesus bade his disciples have a similar wisdom, but *with regard to spiritual matters*, regarding their future. The fact that Jesus used a somewhat disreputable person to make his point does not mean he endorsed what the dishonest steward did. But his choice of a worldly person made his point even more telling. If a son of this world could provide for his (worldly) future, how much more ought people of light to provide for their heavenly future.

Verses 10-13 contain three sayings of Jesus. The first (vs. 10) stated a basic principle about faithfulness and dishonesty. One's character would be the same, regardless of the amount. Increasing the stakes does not change one's inner values. The point is that disciples should be concerned with the inner self and encouraged to faithfulness there. Inner character would result in proper behavior, whether with a penny or with a million dollars.

The second saying (vss. 11f.) was of the "before and after" type. Present wealth was called "unrighteousness mammon" (though probably not implying any intrinsic evil in money) and "that which is another's." The blessings God would give, contingent on the appropriate use of present wealth, was called "true riches" and "that which is your own." Until disciples learn that the money in their pocketbooks, bank accounts, and retirement plans is not theirs, they cannot receive genuine wealth. Jesus taught a radical concept in these words, one that flowed naturally from the recognition that God is Creator, and therefore Possessor, of all.

The third saying (vs. 13) took a recognized truth and

gave it a spiritual application. People in Jesus' day would recognize that a person could not be slave to two masters. Consider, Jesus taught, God and mammon as potential masters. It is axiomatic that God has the right to demand all that a person has (cf. Lk. 17:7-10). But mammon is also demanding, and will make claims like those of the Father: "Know the truth," taught Jesus, "and beware."

LUKE 16:14f.

Because men are so tied to this world and its treasure, teachings like those of Jesus will always be met with scorn by someone. In his time the scorn came from the Pharisees, who were "lovers of money." Jesus responded to their criticism with sharp words: "You are those who justify yourselves before men, but God knows your hearts; for what is exalted among men is an abomination in the sight of God." What more need be said?

LUKE 16:19-31

The familiar story of the rich man and Lazarus, told with such skill, has been used to make many points. But the central point has to do with the compassionate use of wealth. The rich man, who was not named, almost certainly passed many opportunities to provide for the starving man who lay just outside his house (surely not many yards from his dining room). Consequently the rich man went to a place of torment in the afterlife. He had chosen to center on wealth in this life and did not exercise compassion. That choice, when fixed by death, led to tragedy. Though there is a great deal more detail in the story which we might discuss, I believe the central teaching for disciples is use what you have, *now*, while you can, for God's work of compassion. Decisions made in this life do have eternal consequences.

LUKE 18:18-30

This is the other one of the seven stories we are discussing that is not unique to Luke. The ruler who came to Jesus inquired about eternal life (cf. 10:25ff.). At first, Jesus discussed the orthodox answer, referring to the last six of the ten commandments. However, he omitted one, and the ruler would certainly be aware of the omission. It was the command against coveting, and the omission was probably so Jesus could then develop that subject further, since it was the ruler's real problem. In that further development, he told the ruler the way to greater riches ("treasure in heaven," probably equalling eternal life). It was to renounce covetousness by selling all and giving to the poor (cf. 12:33). The ruler, however, seems to have considered treasure in heaven less tangible or less desirable than the wealth he already possessed. There is no indication he accepted the offer, and his sadness (vs. 23) indicates that he did not.

This led to a discussion between Jesus and his disciples about the tenacious hold riches can take on a human life. Jesus described their danger, using the famous needle's eye saying (vs. 23). Despite the difficulty of escaping the clutches of riches, however, the power of God could deliver a person, for what men find impossible God can do.

LUKE 19:1-10

The last of our stories tells of the conversion of Zacchaeus. He was one of the outcasts whom Luke delights in telling readers that Jesus loved. He was so eager to see Jesus he threw dignity to the winds and climbed a tree to glimpse him. Jesus then invited himself into the man's home, where a touching conversion scene follows. Zacchaeus told Jesus he gave half his goods to the poor, and restored fourfold whatever he had taken by fraud. Some argue he was already practicing this lifestyle, and others believe that he changed as a result of the meeting with

Jesus. In either event, he understood that conversion involved, with everything else, the pocketbook. What a contrast between Zacchaeus and the scoffing Pharisees pictured in 16:14f.!

Summary Observations

Jesus' words are so powerful they need little comment. However, let us summarize some of the basic truths unfolded in these texts. We must remember that Jesus did not make up rules about wealth; he spoke about reality. Humans can decide to conform to ultimates—or not. But the truth will not change, regardless of man's attitude toward it. In eternity, we will have to come face to face with our values.

1) Jesus taught that man is not bound to this earth and its satisfactions. No matter what goods one may have, they are never enough to satisfy the deepest human needs. The rich man who built bigger barns and ignored God was called a fool. The Pharisees, the rich man (16:19-31), and the rich ruler all lived out of harmony with the way God had made things. They assumed that something was more important than God. Treasure on earth, no matter how abundant, is not enough.

2) The only real security is in God. Nothing of what God has made can do the job. Those who know where their safety lies are freed from anxiety. They know that if all earthly resources were lost, they would still be within God's loving care. It should be remembered that all forms of wealth and financial security are God's inventions. They exist only because he allows them. He could destroy them whenever he wished. If destroyed, he could re-create them just as he created them in the beginning.

3) When our primary focus is on the riches of this life, we are kept from true riches. It takes faith to believe this

statement is true. But until we have God's riches, we are paupers, regardless of our houses, cars, and investments.

4) Wealth is made to be given. Had the rich man realized this point with regard to Lazarus, his fate would have been different. Zacchaeus grasped this truth. The rich ruler was saddened by the challenge Jesus gave him. Jesus' disciples, secure in their sense of God's care, should sell their possessions and give alms (12:33). Of course, we must not oversimplify matters here, but if we recognize the role of material things in view of God's creative sovereignty, then we can be givers, modeling him the great Giver.

5) A person whose values are wrong cannot enter the kingdom of God. What matters is the inner person. External rules about wealth cannot be made and then followed as if entry were a matter of jumping through the proper hoops. There must be an inner concept of reality.

These premises come from what Jesus said to his disciples. They do not exhaust the conclusions that might be drawn, but at least they provoke us to make personal resolutions about our discipleship. We must remember that Luke was writing to teach about discipleship, just as Jesus was speaking to teach his disciples about the same topic.

In twenty-first century America, where materialism is encouraged on every hand, Luke's message is especially urgent. Even "religious" people (like the Pharisees) can find themselves dominated by material concerns, sometimes without even realizing it. What is needed is a radical consideration of what it means to follow Jesus.

DISCUSSION QUESTIONS

1. If Jesus' disciples were not particularly wealthy, why so much emphasis on this subject in Luke?

2. How is Luke's message about wealth especially relevant in twenty-first century America?

3. What does our American culture teach us about wealth and its acquisition?

4. How can a Christian determine "what percentage to give?"

5. A friend once said, "God wants me to make as much money as I possibly can, so I can use it for him." Do you agree or disagree? Why?

6. How would you apply the story of the rich man and Lazarus to contemporary life? What do you think is the significance of the last part of the story, about the five brothers?

7. Is it possible to be materialistic, and in all other regards be a "good person"—involved in church, Bible reading, prayer, etc.?

8. Have you ever known of a church withdrawing fellowship from someone guilty of greed? Why or why not?

CHAPTER 12
■ Specifics of Discipleship:
The Danger of Faith in Self

In order to practice the aspects of Christian discipleship studied previously in this book, a large measure of humility is necessary. An egotistic, self-centered person cannot practice the kind of love Jesus exhibited and taught. Nor can such a person truly trust God, for he has put self in the place of God as his ultimate object of trust. In order for Jesus' followers to have the proper perspective toward the material world, there must also be a sense of self-denial.

The problem of elevating one's ego above God and making a god of self appears virtually everywhere when we speak of the conduct of disciples. The ordinary people whom Luke shows us in the first two chapters could be used by God because they knew the meaning of submission and humility. Mary, in the great poem often called the *Magnificat* (1:46-55), spoke of God's work. Her words involved the scattering of the proud, the putting down of the mighty, and the exaltation of the lowly. When Jesus first spoke of the seriousness of discipleship, he clearly laid down the lines when he said that those who would save their lives must lose them. The only ones who would be saved were those whose lives were forfeit for the Master's sake (9:24).

We can recall, too, in the series of stories with which Luke ended chapter 9, that we frequently saw his followers caught in the snares of self importance (see especially 9:46-48, 49f., and 51-56). Yet Jesus did not propose to abandon them because of this failing. After all, God even loves the ungrateful and the *selfish*! Yet Jesus was committed to training his followers that they could silence the claims of the self and learn to give as freely as God himself gives.

We have chosen various sample texts to introduce our subject. But for the discerning reader, the problem of the self, and the human temptation to undue personal exaltation, appear in many texts of the gospel.

In the central section of Luke, there are several passages that address our topic. We will notice Jesus' woes against the Pharisees and the lawyers in 11:37-12:1. We will make a brief stop at 19:22f.. We will also note his words about children in 18:15-17 (see the parallel in 9:46-48). Then we must consider two important passages (14:7-11 and 18:9-14), both of which end with the statement, "Every one who exalts himself will be humbled, but he who humbles himself will be exalted."

Finally, slipping beyond the central section, we will note 20:46f., and, from another perspective, 22:24-27.

All of these passages have been indicated here in the beginning, so you can now turn and read them carefully in preparation for further discussion.

The Texts

In contrast to Matthew (who gives them toward the end of the gospel), Luke gives an account of Jesus' woes against the Pharisees and lawyers at an earlier point (11:37-12:1). In the text, Jesus first criticizes the inner uncleanness of the Pharisees, after which he delivers three woes against them (vss. 42, 43, 44). Then, in a verse that seems to have a touch of humor to it, the lawyers did Jesus the favor of giving him the chance to exempt them from his condemnations (v. 45). Jesus declined the opportunity, and instead responded with three woes against the lawyers (vss. 46, 47, 52). For the careful reader, the problems of ego that characterized these religious leaders can be discerned throughout these verses. Thus, when Jesus told his followers to beware of the leaven of the Pharisees, "which is hypocrisy" (12:1), the gist of his words would not have been hard to grasp.

In case the message was unclear (an unlikely case for

any with ears to hear), Jesus made the case even more pointed in Luke 20:46f. There he berated the scribes because they exerted themselves to be in positions where they would be admired and praised. But at the same time, their long prayers were belied by their devouring of widow's houses. Callous robbery of the helpless is a terrible wrong in any situation, but it was particularly worthy of condemnation when covered by a cloak of piety. Those against whom Jesus spoke may have claimed allegiance to God, but it was clear to him that their god was really themselves.

Just before Jesus arrived in Jerusalem, he told the parable of the pounds. Among those to whom the absent master entrusted the safekeeping of a pound was a servant who refused to use what he had been given for his noble lord. For this he was severely condemned, losing even what he had. If this story in Luke 19:11-27 represented the responsibilities of disciples, then the man in question seems to have been so wrapped up in himself that he could not invest on behalf of his master. Jesus commented (vs. 26) that only the willingness to use what one has been given *by* the master *for* the master would lead to greater blessing. In other words, the paradox is that selfishness does not produce gain, as one might think, but rather ensures loss.

The theme of service is expressed in several other contexts. In Luke 18:15-17, Jesus was rebuked by his disciples for receiving and blessing infants. He responded by indicating that the kingdom belonged to such as children. He added that the only way to receive the kingdom was to do so like a child. Even though this passage does not denote any specific characteristic of a child, a similar passage in Matthew 18:4 notes humility as the attribute to be desired.

In this connection, we should note Luke 9:46-48, another case when Jesus took a child to his side. On that occasion he was speaking to followers who had been debating which of them was the greatest. He used his living illustration to teach that greatness would only come to those willing to be the least. One might think that this instruction from Jesus would settle the point. But later his disciples became involved in the very same argument, ironically at the Last Supper (22:24-27), a scene in which the air tingled with the spirit of sacrifice. Perhaps each of Jesus' followers was arguing to show how it would be impossible for him to be the betrayer, of whom Jesus had just spoken (vss. 21f.). Whatever the case, Jesus again made the point that the greatest among his followers must become like the youngest, and the leader must become like one who serves. The point, powerful enough in itself, was driven home by Jesus' statement, "But I am among you as one who serves." These words carry an incredible challenge. If we want to know how strong the claims of ego really are for us humans, we need only reflect that these words are so easily repeated, yet so seldom genuinely practiced.

There are many ways to speak of selfishness and the ego. One is by attending to the matter of humility and pride. Two final passages end with identical sayings about these two topics. In 14:7-11 Jesus observed pride at work in the context of a meal. Some present made sure they would be seated in places of honor, presumably so they would be noticed and praised. Thus Jesus taught about proper behavior at a marriage feast. One should not choose a place of honor, and not only because that would involve the risk of public humiliation if one were forced to a lower seat upon the arrival of a more important person. One should take the lowest place. Even though such a person might have the pleasure of being invited by the host to take a higher seat, Jesus did not mean that the lowest seat should be taken for prideful reasons (sitting there, hoping to be noticed and exalted). Rather, he was saying that in God's governance and judgment of humankind, self-exaltation would produce humiliation (recall 19:22ff.). Those whom God would exalt would be those who voluntarily adopted the posture of humiliation, a willingness to be a selfless servant.

As powerful as this story is, the story of the Pharisee and the publican (18:9-14) may be even stronger. It paints an unforgettable picture, a classic. In addition to the closing statement about exaltation and humility (vs. 14), this text was directed to persons guilty of self-righteousness, those who also despised others. Two sinners went to the temple to pray. One, a Pharisee, did not recognize his sinfulness. Consequently Jesus painted an amusing, but pathetic, picture of a man bragging about his virtues. He even went to the length of describing all the sinners who were beneath him. One, incredibly, was a fellow worshiper—a tax collector. The tax collector, however, had no illusions about himself. He knew he was a sinner, and in deep humility, prayed God to be merciful to him. Of the two, it was the tax collector who was justified, because his choice, the path of humility, meant that God placed him on the high road of exaltation.

(In addition to these last two passages, the same statement about exaltation and humiliation is found in Matthew 23:12.)

Applications

As we have noticed, self-exaltation is the opposite of love and of trust in God. It is, in fact, the basic sin of humanity. In the story of the first sin in Eden, the offer to the woman was aimed directly at her ego. She was given the chance to have her eyes opened—to be like God. She could assume, it appeared, complete control of her life. She could become her own deity. In the simple act of eating the forbidden fruit, God was dethroned in her life, and she was enthroned—except that it did not really happen that way, for self-deification is a contradiction to the nature of reality, and one who deifies self can only suffer defeat.

Yet since that first sin, every sin committed in the history of the world, even to this very day, including all of yours and mine, has been a form of self-deification. When we sin, we decide that what we want is more important than anything else. No other voice than our own speaks with greater authority in determining how we will live. We may not consider our wrongs—even our little ones—sp rebellious but, upon analysis, that is exactly what they are.

This self-rule takes many forms. It can surface in the life of a person of whom all acquaintances may say, "that person is extremely selfish." Supply your own names. It may appear as a form of stubbornness. Of course, I recognize the value of strong conviction in areas where compromise is unthinkable for a Christian. But anyone who has observed life for long can see the difference between the two.

The closed mind, unwilling to consider and to learn, is another symptom of this spiritual disease. Self-pity, because it is always focused on "me," is yet another way the problem surfaces. Then there is pride, in its myriad forms. Manipulativeness is a further manifestation. Manipulators operate only for their own advantage, regardless of the cost to others. Even minor instances of inconsideration display the dominance of self.

These, of course, are only samples. If they have set your mind to working, you can no doubt think of many more places where egocentricity has broken out, both in general terms and in specific cases. But by far the most important thing is to see the problem in our own lives, and to engage in the proper spiritual exercises to help in conquering it.

In C. S. Lewis' adult fantasy entitled *The Great Divorce*, a tour group travels from hell to heaven. The hellish ghosts were met by bright heavenly spirits who had come infinite distances from deep heaven to beg the damned souls to stay in heaven rather than return to hell. Though scripture teaches that judgment fixes an impassible gulf between the two places, Lewis uses this device to make some powerful spiritual points. One of the main emphases of the book is the importance of choice; of all the characters who received impassioned pleas to remain in heaven, only one accepted. When the reader asks why they refused, analysis shows that in each case pride was central. Those declining heaven's love song simply could not submit themselves to

God's mercy. Self was so settled in the center of their lives that it could not be dethroned. So, by means of this fantasy, Lewis challenges his readers to choose the proper object to worship—while that choice can still be made. This is what Jesus was teaching his disciples. This is what all disciples must learn.

DISCUSSION QUESTIONS

1. How does Jesus' teaching about humility relate to various self-actualization theories and psychological techniques encountered today?

2. How are religious leaders tempted to pride (11:37-12:1)?

3. Why is selfishness self-defeating?

4. Many consider self-centeredness the basic human sin, forming the background for all other sins. Do you agree? Justify your answer. Is self-love the root of all sins?

5. What are the more subtle ways even "good" people can be self-centered?

6. Are humans basically good, as some claim, or basically evil? Explain your answer.

7. How can people in positions of importance or power, who receive the attention or adulation of others, avoid the worship of self?

CHAPTER 13
■ Blessings of Discipleship

I have pointed out the inadequacies and needs of those disciples whom Jesus was training. We have not considered the issue of whether or not they thought it worth following him. However, when we examine the gospel, that does not seem to have been an issue. Though they were far from what they should have been, nowhere does the central section indicate they considered any option other than completing the decision they made when they first began to follow him. They didn't give up on him. More importantly, he didn't give up on them.

Yet modern man, thinking as he does, often asks the questions of any proposed course of action, "Is it worth it? What's in it for me?" When we address such questions, we come to consider the blessings of discipleship. Jesus spoke of these blessings on numerous occasions as he traveled to Jerusalem.

When we think the matter through, however, the question "Is it worth it?" can quite easily get us on the wrong track. It may imply a bargain, a transaction in which we have something to offer God. We decide whether or not we will give that something, depending on what we might get in return. The question may also imply that a large enough reward might even lead us to pursue an otherwise unattractive course in order to reap the greater benefits at the end of the period of unpleasantness. Of course, neither of these possibilities reflects the reality of following Jesus, even though one often finds Christians whose view of the faith operates from these mistaken assumptions.

In our discussion, we must remember the story of the unworthy servant, told by Jesus in Luke 17:7-10. In the story the servant, coming in from a hard day's labor, was expected to serve the master before attending to his own needs. Even then the master was not expected to thank him, since the servant was only doing his duty. Humans are the servants and God is the master. He is our creator and sustainer. Nothing we have is our own. We have nothing to give him that was not his to begin with. Surrendering all we are to him is only logical and appropriate, since we are total debtors, whether we recognize it or not. There is no question of bargaining with God about whether or not we will be disciples; we have nothing with which to bargain. Further, God made us for joy, and joy is found only in relationship to him. There is no question of following an unpleasant path in hope of eventual reward. The very following is sheer joy, even if it should bring suffering (a paradox non-Christians find difficult to comprehend).

Let us turn, then, to Jesus' words, hearing them again as addressed to Jesus' companions, to Luke's readers, and to us, his most recent followers.

The Texts

Luke 10:17-20. The seventy whom Jesus sent to preach and heal returned from their mission with joy. While commenting on the wonder of the exorcisms they had performed, Jesus said, "Rejoice that your names are written in heaven." I take this to be a blessing offered to all faithful disciples, indicating that such people are acknowledged and remembered by their Creator.

Luke 10:23f. After praying, Jesus told his disciples they were blessed even more than the prophets and kings of old because of what they had seen and heard. They were participating in the desire of the ages—the most important point of history. They were among those who really knew the meaning of the parade of human events through the centuries.

Luke 11:1-13. In this classic prayer passage, Jesus assured his followers of God's concern for them. Indeed, he urged them to pray, promising to answer. The text of the model prayer (vss. 2b-4) indicates the essential human needs to which God promises to respond.

Luke 11:27f. When a woman in the crowd blessed the mother of Jesus, he responded by indicating that blessing was rather for those who heard the word of God and kept it. Obedient response was considered a greater treasure than the physical motherhood of Jesus.

Luke 12:6f. In this context, Jesus' disciples were instructed regarding persecution. In such times, Jesus said, they could be sure of God's care. If even an insignificant sparrow was remembered by God, how much more would his disciples be remembered. Even the hairs of their heads were numbered by him. The blessing was that disciples would never be forsaken, no matter how terrible the circumstances.

Luke 12:8f. Immediately following the assurance that they could not be forsaken, Jesus promised that those who acknowledged him before men, presumably when persecuted, would be acknowledged by the Son of Man before the angels of heaven.

Luke 12:24, 29-31. In these verses Jesus assured his followers that they need not worry about life's material needs. God, who knew their needs, would see to it that they were supplied with food, drink, and clothing.

Luke 12:33. Immediately following the promise of material needs, Jesus called his disciples to sell—willingly—their possessions and give to the poor. They would be blessed with treasure in heaven, which would not be subject to destruction or theft.

Luke 12:37. In this parable of the servants faithfully waiting for the master to return from the marriage feast, those who were faithful were blessed by being served by the master. If Jesus was speaking of the second coming, the point would be that those ready for his return would receive his blessings.

Luke 12:44. In another illustration encouraging readiness for the Lord's return, Jesus promised that the faithful steward would be set over all the master's possessions.

Luke 13:29. Jesus pictured the end of the age with the image of a banquet. The faithful were blessed by being seated at table in the kingdom of God. Others, who might have expected to be seated there, were excluded, to their terrible anguish.

Luke 14:12-14. Jesus pronounced those blessed who did good works (gave a banquet) for people because they were in need, rather than just for what they could get in return. Though the poor could not repay the feast giver, the host would be repaid at the resurrection of the just.

Luke 16:9, 11f. The story of the dishonest steward was concluded with Jesus' promise of eternal habitations for the people of the light who used their "unrighteous mammon" properly. Then, in a collection of sayings about the use of wealth, Jesus contrasted goods of this world with the ultimate blessings that would come from God. These latter he called "true riches" and "that which is your own."

Luke 18:1-8. Here Jesus promised that God would hear the prayers of his elect and would vindicate them "speedily" (a problematic word, but probably indicating that God's action, when it came, would be decisive).

Luke 18:29f. The rich ruler, with whom Jesus was speaking in this text, had asked the way to eternal life. In the end of the passage, Jesus told his disciples that they would not only receive "manifold more in this time"— house, wife, brothers, parents, and children—but in the age to come would receive eternal life. (Note, too, the discussion about eternal life in 10:25ff.)

Luke 19:26. In the parable of the pounds the faithful subject of the king was promised he would receive greater riches than he already possessed. The point seems to be that God would multiply blessings that had been used for him.

Systematization

It appears that many of the statements just examined are of a general nature; they don't indicate the specific nature of the blessing to be granted the disciple. However, this isn't always the case. There are specific blessings indicated. The disciple knows the meaning of history (10:23f.). The blessing of prayer is of enormous importance (11:1-13; 18:7f.), an importance amplified by the role we see prayer play in the life of Jesus throughout Luke (cf. 3:21; 5:16; 6:12; 9:16, 18, 28; 10:21; 11:1; 22:17, 19, 42, 44; 23:34, 46; and 24:30). We should also notice the Holy Spirit as a blessing accompanying prayer (11:13). Perhaps this text is indicating that the Spirit is the power by which God answers prayer.

The disciple also has the present promise of knowing that material needs will be supplied (12:31), which is part of the larger promise of God's constant and intimate love and care (12:4-7).

But many of the passages speak of the future, employing a rich variety of images. What is the core meaning of all these references? Maybe the greatest blessing, implicit in all that Jesus said, is fellowship with God. He has made us. He is the author of all joy, all happiness, all blessedness. Only he can perfectly supply the needs that he built into us by his creative power. We may not be able to comprehend the greatness of this blessedness, but we should believe it and realize that richness beyond imagining awaits us if we are faithful. If a man has fellowship with God, what greater bliss could possibly be added? What, without God, could give even an instant of genuine happiness?

We should beware of making too fine a distinction between present and future, between earth and heaven. God's blessings are present in real form for the disciple in this life. They are not antithetical to what is to come. If the richness now is almost more than we can stand, how much greater will that be which is yet to come? The process of blessing is not awaiting the future to begin. It is working in the *present* of the follower of Jesus—even, strangely enough, when the immediate physical circum-stances of life are most miserable. Is discipleship worth it? The real question is, "Is any other lifestyle worth it?" No reward is

103

really great enough to induce us to abandon the very purpose for which God made us—to know God and to enjoy him forever.

A Final Word

These statements about the blessing of discipleship complete the program mapped out for our study of Luke's central section. They don't close the issue of discipleship in Luke/Acts, however. Did the disciples learn from what Jesus taught them? From an investigation of the later chapters of Luke, it would appear not. Careful examination of chapter 22 shows the disciples failing just as miserably as we noticed them failing in chapter 9. Chapter 24, the resurrection chapter, indicates more of the same. There, they—four times!—disbelieved that Jesus had been raised (vss. 11, 16, 37, 41).

But in Acts 2 God sent the Holy Spirit. In the subsequent chapters we see a remarkable change, as the disciples' lives were empowered by God's Spirit. Two examples are particularly powerful: Peter's courageous defense in Acts 4:8-12 (contrast his denial in Luke 22:54-62) and John's work with the Samaritans in Acts 8:17 (contrast Luke 9:51-56).

It is not easy to learn to be a disciple. There are many failures. But God is patient with us—more patient than we are inclined to be with ourselves. And he offers us his power, to make of us what we cannot become by ourselves. That is the central message of discipleship.

DISCUSSION QUESTIONS

1. On what basis does Jesus have the right to ask "everything" of us?

2. Is Luke 12:33 an absolute command for all time, or is it a principle that can be followed even without literal obedience?

3. How do you reconcile Jesus' statements in chapter 12 about material needs being supplied with the fact that some Christians in the world go hungry? Is it possible that the promise of the supply of food and clothing is not real—or the deepest—meaning of the passage?

4. In what way has fellowship with God brought blessings to your life?

5. Besides the examples of Peter and John, how do you see the themes of discipleship demonstrated in Acts?

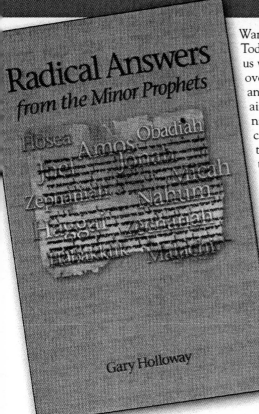